PRAISE FOR *Finding Deep and Wide*

"I don't know what a cathead biscuit is, but I do know Shellie loves the Lord and His Word. Her obvious Southern charm draws you in like a moth to the front porch light. Shellie challenges the reader to peel away religious rhetoric and trade 'less than' living and 'I'll follow Him later' mindsets for a relationship like none other—a 'more than' life and 'I'll follow Him anywhere' attitude. Grab a glass of sweet tea and sit with your new friend Shellie Tomlinson."

Wendy Pope
Speaker and author of *Wait and See, Yes, No and Maybe*, and *Hidden Potential*

"Life feels so serious so much of the time. And then along comes Shellie Rushing Tomlinson, delivering exactly what I need. Go deeper with Jesus? Yes! I'm in! Go deeper and wider with snorts, smiles and hoots of laughter? Even better! There's nothing trivial in the fun of this profound book."

Leslie Leyland Fields
Author of *Your Story Matters: Finding, Writing and Living the Truth of Your Life*

"When I think of Shellie Tomlinson, I think of the night we stayed up late talking about the twists and turns of a hard, complicated life and how Jesus met us there. I can tell you this: Shellie loves Jesus like a boat loves water. And every time I'm with her, I end up loving Jesus more, too. When you read *Finding Deep and Wide*, you will feel like you've stayed up late with a bestie and talked about the most important things in life. Even better, by the time you close the last page of this book, you'll have new tools to help you live the deep and wide life you were created for."

Michele Cushatt
Author of *Relentless: The Unshakeable Presence of a God Who Never Leaves*

"In *Finding Deep and Wide*, Shellie Tomlinson, in true Shellie form, entertains, inspires and challenges us to discover just how much God loves us and wants the best for us. Through her captivating stories set *deep* in the heart of Louisiana, Shellie teaches us how to open our hearts *wide* and experience a love like no other. Pour a cup of coffee or a glass of sweet tea, drink in the words of this book, and truly fill your spirit with everything God wants for you."

Chrys Howard
Author of *Rockstar Grandparent*

"Anyone who has ever had the immeasurable Joy of Jesus Christ pierce through their veins has also shed tears of sorrow over loved ones that yawn over this same Jesus. Why do some worship and some yawn? *Finding Deep and Wide* provides a loving and humorous Holy Spirit-led pathway to bridge this chasm, offering heartfelt encouragement along the way. Shellie offers practical and time-tested advice rooted in Scripture for all those who desire to move from tiresome religion to a life-giving, deep and wide, 24/7, Jesus-loving faith. This book is a true treasure that will help lead you into the very presence of almighty God."

Todd Steward
President
Gulf Winds International

"Imagine having a friend who could help you discover the secret to the over-the-top Christian life you've been craving. Shellie is that fried. Religious duty versus passionate devotion to Christ? Shellie Tomlinson has lived both ways. Since she uncovered the secret to freedom from 'less-than living,' she's been committed to helping others find the way. Take Shellie's hand as she guides you down the path (and through some of her LOL-crazy antics) toward what your heart's been craving—wholehearted devotion to Christ. *Finding Deep and Wide* is a fun book filled with great stories to help you grasp biblical, life-changing principles. You'll discover practical ways to live so in love with Jesus that He becomes your everything. This is a great, easy-to-read book that you can read alone or with a group study—with thought-provoking questions at the end of each chapter. I pray God uses this book to light your fire and guide you toward the over-the-top life you crave. Well done Shellie! This book is sure to be a favorite."

Rhonda Stoppe
Author of *Moms Raising Sons to Be Men* and *The Marriage Mentor*

"Few authors can so seamlessly weave powerful quotes, clear illustrations, compelling stories from Scripture, and even her own experiences into a powerful picture of a faith-filled life well-lived. Shellie Tomlinson does it well and makes it seem effortless! Shellie not only writes powerfully, she authentically lives powerfully as one who is searching for and 'finding deep and wide' in her everyday life. This book calls us away from the false choice between the secular and the sacred and instead invites us to experience God's grace, presence and pleasure in all of it. *Finding Deep and Wide* will change your life for the spiritually richer, healthier, and better if you let it!"

Jonathan Wiggins
Lead Pastor
Rez Church, Loveland, Colorado

Finding Deep & Wide

Finding Deep & Wide

Stop Settling for the Life You Have and Live the One Jesus Died to Give You

Shellie Rushing Tomlinson

SALEM
BOOKS

an imprint of Regnery Publishing

Contents

To The Fabulous Five:

EMERSON, GRANT, CARLISLE, CONNOR, AND WESTON

How often you ask me to hold
a precious treasure while you play.
I pray you'll live understanding the only way
to keep your lives is to let Jesus hold them.
Love, "Keggie"

Introduction

I grew up taking long summer road trips with my parents and my two older sisters. My siblings and I were a backseat trio of discontented warriors, arguing, fussing, and whining, "Are we there yet?"

My papa was famous for his don't-worry-be-happy responses. "We're on vacation," he'd say. "And we're going to have fun whether you like it or not. You girls had best act like you're enjoying yourselves!"

We girls were adept at complying because we really did know what was good for us, but we were actresses putting on a happy face because it was expected of us, not because we were truly joyful.

Believers often do this. While agreeing that living with God in our midst—in our very bodies, at that—should work us up into the type of daily celebration the prophet Isaiah spoke about when he said, *"Cry aloud and shout for joy, O inhabitant of Zion, For great in your midst is the Holy One of Israel!"* (Isaiah 12:6 NASB), we accept a substandard experience of what it means to carry the Hope of Glory around in these all-too-human vessels. We settle for only *acting* like having new life in Christ is something to shout about.

I call it "less-than" living.

I first met Jesus while seated in a little bitty chair in a small country church singing "Deep and Wide." He was perfect, and I was nowhere close. (I figured that out early enough.) I loved everything they told me about Invisible Jesus. As I grew up, I decided I wanted to follow Him even though I wasn't sold on living exclusively for Him. This translated into trying to appease God while I lived to please me. I also understood rule-keeping, regardless of how often I failed at it. "If at first you don't succeed," right?

Even after I grew discontented with the distance between me and Jesus and decided I wanted to know Him like the Bible said I could, I kept trying to get there in the only way I knew—through my best efforts. It wasn't a conscious decision. Raised on God's Word and cathead biscuits, I knew I couldn't "finish in the flesh" what the author of Galatians tells us "had begun in the Spirit," but I soon fell into the wearying cycle of knuckling down to measure up, always trying to gauge how pleased God was with me to decide how welcome I was with Him. Performing exhausted me, and it didn't lead me any closer to what had become my heart's desire—knowing Him more.

Thankfully, I'm discovering the joy of dying to all that trying. These days, I'm learning to live in what Jesus has already done, and I'm finding that all Jesus promised lives at the end of me. It is the deep and wide life Scripture has always told me I could have.

And here's the thing: quitting never felt so good! I haven't mastered quitting. I should get that out there before we go any further. That said, I'm learning how to quit on me and live in Jesus, and our shared journey has become so fulfilling, so flat-out precious that I'd like to pause and invite you to join us. That's what this book is all about.

I don't have all the answers—not even close—but I can show you the way Holy Spirit has brought me: in learning to live dying, in denying my will and choosing His, in being transformed as I behold Jesus. All Jesus, no me. All grace, no merit. This glory, that Jesus does all the heavy lifting as we yield and keep our eyes on Him, is where I pray this book will lead us all—into the deep and wide life available in Christ Jesus. My not-so-secret goal is to make you crazy hungry for the way of life God wants for you, planned for you, and paid the ultimate cost to provide for you.

Our journey will take us through both the Old and New Testaments as we look at heroes of the faith who knew what it was to experience the deep and wide relationship with God that He intended all of us to have from the get-go. I'll show you why we so often miss it and discuss some healthy heart habits that will help us get back in on it!

Come with me. I dare you.

Shellie Rushing Tomlinson
January 2020

Chapter One

. . . . .

Y'all Come Back Now, Ya Hear?

"Absolute seriousness is never without a dash of humor."

—DIETRICH BONHOEFFER

I had just enjoyed a sanity-saving, soul-satisfying talk with Jesus on my lakeside dock when I checked the time. Bummer. It was getting late early. It's probably best if I don't go into why I'd lingered in prayer longer than usual, lest I scare you off in the first paragraph. But I can give you the condensed version: I had to stay after class for extra counseling on my attitude. It can get sideways on days that end in "y," and I don't mind owning that I've discovered that Jesus is silky-smooth about helping a person straighten up and fly right. It's kind of like the family business for Him.

I had intended to take a morning kayak ride on beautiful Lake Providence, but the sun had climbed high in the sky, and everything that needed doing before it set again ran through my thoughts. It made more sense to head to the shower—but things that make more sense seldom rule the day around here.

And that's how I came to be paddling down the lake mid-morning, even though our Louisiana summer was in full swing and it was already H-O-T hot. (My people would say "hotter than H-E-Double L," and that would not be cussing cause because they spelled it, but again, I'm trying to put my best foot forward in these early pages.)

Backstory? My custom is to give the aged cypress trees lining the lake banks a healthy berth because God could've wiped snakes off the planet back in the Garden, but no, He chose to let them live (flourish even, at least here in the Louisiana Delta), and I've grown up hearing stories of snakes falling out of trees and into the boats of the unsuspecting. It happened to my late Papaw once. He and his good friend Marvin Nichols were fishing one day when Papaw's buddy up and jumped straight into the water and began swimming for shore with Olympic speed.

"What in tarnation are you doing?" Papaw yelled.

Mr. Nichols hollered over his shoulder without losing a beat in his breaststroke, "Snake in the boat! Snake in the boat!"

I must commend Papaw. He forgave his buddy for going with the "each man for himself" philosophy. He and Mr. Nichols went on to fish together many a day. Let the record show, if something like that ever happened to me, I'd try walking on the water, *à la* our biblical friend Peter.

Yet, despite this well-documented snake phobia of mine, there I was hugging the tree line closer than usual because, again, Louisiana summer heat and possible shade. It's the only reason I heard that first weak whimper.

It was a hoarse cry, so faint it took me a second to locate the source. But once I did, I found a heart-wrenching sight. A foot or so from the lake bank, a small white dog was balancing on a knot of several cypress knees and whimpering for help. (It may seem strange to refer to the knee of a tree, but it's a common reference to the root-like structures that form around our bald cypress trees. They resemble cones and tend to grow in clusters.) Behind the desperate canine were the remains of an old sea wall from which he had undoubtedly fallen. As I took in the scene, the puppy's wails grew louder and more insistent. He turned, scratched at the sea wall, and looked back, as if to say, "See? I can't get up!"

Indeed, regardless of how high he stretched, the puppy's reach fell about two feet shy of the wall's top shelf. It'd be impossible for him to gather his feet under him and jump to freedom. I studied his predicament and stalled for time. Who knows how long he'd been marooned on that knot of cypress knees? I mean, he was thin as a rail, but that can happen to a puppy that goes without food for even a day or two.

Clearly, this guy's problem had now become my own, and I didn't like where things were headed. The pitiful puppy wasn't stranded at the edge of someone's yard. That would've been too easy. Puppy was marooned in what I refer to as alligator land, a swampy run of lake bank with wild overgrown brush, most likely harboring every species of snake in Louisiana. (Not to belabor the point, Lord, but we do have more than our fair share.)

Going in after the distraught puppy would require maneuvering around the rusty, nail-studded remains of a dilapidated dock and under the overhanging vines and drooping limbs of a group of cypress trees. Oh, joy.

I pulled out my smart phone for a quick picture and put it away just as quickly. I wasn't in my customary "I must document this for social media" mode—a fact that amazes my husband and kids to this day because they contend I don't let a moment of our lives go undocumented. While they may have a collective point, I feel they should be more grateful and less snippy about my commitment to the role of family historian, so there you go. I simply knew the image would fail to do the scene justice. It'd be hard to grasp the depth between the trees, those snaky-looking vines, and the lake bank without being there, but trust me. It was creepy times two.

I briefly tried to cajole the panicked puppy into swimming toward me. Dear reader, I imagine your eyes rolling here, but desperate people don't always think clearly. That said, Puppy would have agreed with you. He wailed even louder. I interpreted his response as something like, "Silly woman, I'm not about to get in that water!"

Confession. The following question crossed my mind: "What would Red and Carey do?" That would be my best friend (Red, aka Rhonda) and my daughter-in-law. They're both big-time dog lovers. I felt sure neither of them would be hesitating like yours truly was doing. However, in my defense, my thought process wasn't nearly as lengthy as it sounds. It only took a minute or ten to convince myself that, deep sigh, I was going in after the stranded puppy. God has this way of bringing Scripture back to my mind at *just* the right time ...

Remember that at that time you were separate from Christ, excluded from citizenship in Israel and foreigners to the covenants of the promise, without hope and without God in the world (Ephesians 2:12 NIV).

Without hope. That was Puppy.

The rescue was even more difficult and scary than I imagined, and I had the makings of a bad movie going on in my head. As the canopy of limbs grew thicker above me, it's possible I began beseeching Heaven with considerably more passion than I had during my earlier devotion. I was suddenly a world-class prayer warrior. *"Oh, God, puullleeeassse don't let a snake fall in this kayak with me, please, please, please, please ..."*

All the while, I was drawing closer to the frantic puppy—whose cries had risen in direct proportion to my proximity. I don't know what I expected his reaction to be in response to my compassionately courageous and heroically self-sacrificing rescue efforts. (Too thick?) I can only assure you I was not at all prepared for what happened. Would you believe the hairy little refugee was so out of his mind with fear that once I finally drew near enough to reach for him, he tried to bite me?! Me! His brave belle in the sweaty tank top!

I am trying to save your scrawny neck here, I thought to myself. *Work with me, Puppy!*

"My people are bent on turning from me." (Hosea 11.7 NASB)

Now, the thing about a half-dead puppy balanced on cypress knees is that it can't actually be balanced. It was easy enough to distract the angry mutt—I mean, the poor darling—with one hand long enough to snatch him up by the nape of his scrawny neck and deposit him in the kayak with the other.

Grateful he was not.

The drenching wet sack of bones assumed a defensive stance and commenced to growling and baring his pearly-white puppy teeth with as much aggression as he could muster.

You're quite welcome. It was nothing. No, really.

I had no choice but to ignore my hysterical passenger as I tried to back my kayak out of swampy alligator habitat and snake land and point it toward home. Meanwhile, my guest chose to crawl to the front of our vessel and bury his face as far in the hull as he could stuff it.

As I paddled home, I began soothing the little guy in that voice we all use with babies and puppies. His response was to tuck his tail beneath his body and wedge himself even further into the hull.

Fine, then.

I abandoned the sweet talk and began to sing over him. I'll admit my vocals have never calmed a single despondent human, but they seemed to work reasonably well on my new canine friend. At the very least, he quit whimpering. So I sang, paddled, and thought of an Old Testament verse that depicted God singing like me.

The Lord your God in your midst, The Mighty One, will save; He will rejoice over you with gladness, He will quiet you with His love, He will rejoice over you with singing (Zephaniah 3:17 NKJV).

Some twenty minutes later, as we neared my dock, Puppy and I faced the next challenge in our shaky relationship in the form of

Dixie Belle, my beloved chocolate Lab, who was already barking loud enough to wake the dead, as my people say. My self-appointed guardian had long gone on record as being uncomfortable with my early-morning kayak rides, and now I was returning with a soaking wet puppy that looked more like a scared possum. (Dixie has since gone to Heaven because all dogs do, but I'm still not over her. So that's all we'll say about that.)

I whispered yet another prayer for divine assistance. The last thing I needed was for the traumatized puppy in my kayak to dive overboard trying to get away from Dixie and create yet more drama for us all. For once, Dixie complied when I quieted her. (I still think that qualifies as an official miracle.) I wish I could say the puppy was as cooperative about transitioning to the dock. Negative. I was forced to proceed to plan B once it became obvious he wasn't budging from the hull without burying his sharp baby teeth in my hands. After manhandling the kayak, puppy and all, out of the water and onto the dock, I pulled the vessel up our sloping back yard and parked it under the oak tree.

I spent the next few minutes doing more of the soothing-voice thing. This got me exactly nowhere, although the refugee did turn and look at me over his shoulder several times as his eyes grew noticeably heavy, suggesting the sole thing he wanted after his harrowing ordeal was a good long nap. It sounded good to me, too, but work was calling.

I rustled up some dog food, poured a little water in a bowl, and put the nourishment near the puppy in the kayak, figuring once I was out of the picture, he wouldn't have to venture more than a few inches if he chose to eat. Satisfied I'd done all I could, I headed inside to shower and get my day started.

I thought about Mercy while I was getting dressed. By now, I had given him what I considered to be the most obvious name under the circumstances, because nothing but M-E-R-C-Y could have prompted me to go where I went to rescue him. (And yes, I do realize "Mercy" sounds more like a girl's name, but it fit.)

He saved us, not on the basis of deeds which we have done in righteousness, but according to his mercy ... (Titus 3:5 NASB)

By the time I'd completed my extreme makeover—another story we don't have time for—I had decided Mercy was a gift in disguise. Dixie Belle was getting older than I wanted to think about, and this puppy would always remind me of God's great mercy. (Doesn't that sound neat? I thought so, too.) Imagine my surprise when I slipped back out to check on Mercy and found he had disappeared. A bite or two of food was gone, and so was my refugee!

Then Jesus answered and said, "Were there not ten cleansed? But the nine—where are they? Was no one found who returned to give glory to God, except this foreigner?" (Luke 17:17-18 NASB)

I thought about Mercy the rest of that day. I looked for him on my trips to and from town, hoping I wouldn't find his lifeless little body on the road. I was convinced Mercy was gone for good, but the very next morning, he showed up on our back porch around the same time I'd rescued him the day before. He was still whimpering and covered in fleas. He may have been covered in fleas the day before, but if you'll recall, I wasn't allowed to examine him before he made his great escape.

Day Two found Mercy a tad more willing to make nice than he was at our first meet and greet. He still nipped at me, but with a tad less aggression. Slowly, I earned his trust enough to feed him. That was a scene, but once I pried his mouth open and put a finger dripping with the dog-food gravy directly on his black and pink tongue, we began to make progress. Mercy licked his lips and looked at me with something approaching appreciation, or at the very least, concealed distrust.

Soon my little refugee was allowing me to run my hands over his body to check for injuries. From there, he found himself getting dipped for fleas and being forced to undergo an ear rinse with Dixie's ear-mite meds. Once again, he opted for a post-drama nap. I had no idea what the next day would bring, but at least for that moment, Mercy was safe and sound.

Mercy's arms-length appreciation spoke to me. As I watched him curl into an ultra-sensitive ball of fur, my thoughts turned to God's amazing grace and how He lovingly pursues us. I remembered how willing I once was to grasp the eternal redemption God offered while being wary of what else He might expect of me. I grabbed at the forever home He held out, but I hesitated to embrace His invitation for deeper relationship. For starters, I had no idea how to take Him up on it. But that's the sanitized version. The whole truth? I didn't care to try.

Living the Lie

Oh, I'd been in church all my life. I knew I wanted to be on God's good side come Judgment Day, but I spent years feeling like I was devoting enough time to Him in the pew and in my daily Bible reading (extra points, y'all!) without having my entire life absorbed into some kind of sub-par religious pursuit where I thought I'd have to give up all hope of getting what I thought I wanted out of life and forfeit all the fun stuff.

Did you hear a lot of "me, myself, and I" there? I'm sure God did, too. It's ugly but true. Conflicted as to what a present-tense, ongoing relationship with God might require of me, I came and went to His throne like Mercy the Refugee, trying to get my needs met without giving up my independence. Today, I'd tell you my deepest fulfillment has been discovering He is my greatest need.

For whoever wishes to save his life will lose it; but whoever loses his life for My sake will find it. (Matthew 16:25 NASB)

But I'm getting ahead of myself.

As I watched this traumatized stray quivering in his sleep, his wariness tugged at tender places in my heart. I knew I wouldn't be able to love Mercy the way I wanted to if he insisted on running away. I also knew I'd love him more than he could possibly imagine if he chose to stay.

The chasm between my love for Mercy and his inability to return it was all too familiar. But I'll leave the analogy there and pray it's served its purpose. The journey I'm inviting you to share is an ongoing story about what begins to happen once we quit treating God like a halfway house. There'll be plenty of hard-earned, transparent, and ongoing experience from me, but I believe there's also life-transforming value here for you.

For indeed, I did quit running back and forth to God. Eventually.

The season came when I began to long for more than just believing in God and knowing *about* Jesus. I wanted the relationship the Bible said was available. The goal lines of my life were moving. Ironically, I'd need to learn a lot more about quitting as I raced toward Jesus, for a whole new trap had been set for me—and for the longest time, I was clueless as to why I kept tripping!

But we'll get to that soon enough. For now, I think it's more important for us to unpack the big lie that kept me holding God at what I thought was a comfortable distance for so long. Why? Because I had bought the big lie, and you may have, too.

Questions for Group Study or Private Reflection

1. On a scale of 0-10, how satisfying is your faith walk?
2. What could it mean to treat God like a halfway house?
3. Shellie admits to buying a big lie. Before you turn the page, take a guess at the nature of the lie. (There are no wrong answers!)

Chapter Two

. . . . .

Giving Up Our Fleas

"There is no key to happiness; the door is always open."

—MOTHER TERESA

The teenage boy talking to me wasn't mine, but I loved him like my own. He was a high school junior and my son's buddy—but since Phillip wasn't home that afternoon when his friend dropped by, I was acting as a somewhat startled sounding board for more information than I could've anticipated. Years later, I still remember the details of our conversation, including the grin on his face and the twinkle in his eyes.

Sam (not his real name) was on the outs with his mama. He knew she was worried about him because he wasn't "following God." That's a summary of what we'd been talking about when Sam announced without apology that he believed in God but that he had his whole life ahead of him and he wanted to have fun now and do the God thing later.

I wanted to counter Sam's argument, but I wasn't sure what to say. At the time, I wasn't long removed from my own "I'll follow Him later" thinking, and I was still taking baby steps toward understanding how to let God be more to me than a fire insurance policy. So I understood his reluctance more than he could've imagined, but being the adult in the room (term used loosely), I felt compelled to maximize this opportunity to help him see the light.

I fell back on sermons I'd heard all my life, with heavy emphasis on how Sam couldn't count on coming to Jesus later because none of us know when our turn is up, and he could have a four-wheeler accident on the way home and not live through it. (Right. That's about the same impression my speech had on Sam.) He made a fast getaway, and I didn't blame him. My version of a come-to-Jesus meeting had all the appeal of a root canal.

I'd have a better answer for Sam today. I'd tell him how I once felt that same way, but I've discovered Jesus is everything I thought I was holding out for—and more. I'd tell him about the deep need Jesus meets in me, and how I'm learning to let Him meet it. In short, I wouldn't try to change Sam; I'd tell Sam about Jesus changing me. And I'd trust Jesus to do what He wanted with my words ... without a morbid four-wheeler illustration.

Maybe you can identify with Sam's blatant honesty. Maybe you're still secretly wary of what you think God wants from you, too. But what God wants for us far outstrips what we're after for ourselves, and I intend to prove that to you. Much as I wanted to nurture Mercy beyond our dramatic rescue, God wants to do more for you and me (and Sam!) than save us from an eternity without Him. His plan to save us can't be separated from His desire to reveal Himself to us because eternal life and knowing God are one and the same.

This is eternal life, that they may know You, the only true God, and Jesus Christ whom you have sent (John 17:3 NASB).

In Christ, God gave us Himself. There's no greater gift.

This is how God showed his love among us: He sent his one and only Son into the world that we might live through him (1 John 4:9 NIV).

So why do we act like wary refugees reluctant to totally give up our perceived independence, even if what we see as freedom comes with fleas? Maybe because we've grown accustomed to them. They're our fleas, after all. We'll live with a lot of pesky problems and less-than-desirable situations if we think we're in charge. Or at least until it becomes unbearable.

Back when I thought God was after my whole life (and He was, but stay with me), I pretty much resented Him for it. I wouldn't have admitted this to another soul, but I figured if I was regularly checking off the Good Christian Woman box—church attendance, Bible reading, morning prayer list—I deserved time off from God for good behavior. I felt like my life in between such spiritual activities was my own until it was time to check in with God again. You know, kind of like the relationship a parolee has with a parole officer. (I understand if you winced at that. It wasn't fun to type either, but I'm committed to dragging ugly into the light where we can all get a good look at it.)

To clarify, I didn't consciously want to disobey God as much as I wanted to protect time and space for me, Shellie—keeping a place where my "want-to" still mattered. I thought I was holding onto my freedom, that's all. What I didn't realize was this determination to preserve "me space" in my life was bondage masquerading as individual liberty. Worse, my choice to hold onto some version of my own independence from God was keeping me from the full, adventurous, satisfying life I thought I was protecting. Irony of ironies.

I had fallen for the big lie. The big sad lie.

The late theologian C. S. Lewis says it this way, "When we try to keep within us an area that is our own, we try to keep an area of death. Therefore, in love, He claims all. There's no bargaining with Him" (*The Weight of Glory, and Other Addresses*, 1980).

God's invitation is so much bigger than mere rescue because life is God's idea and He wants to experience it *with* us. You and I were never meant to travel through this world without His Presence, toughing it out all by our lonesome. Our good Father intended to share our waking-up, sitting-down, pleasant, painful, joyful, mournful, exhilarating, and exhausting moments. He longs for us to see they're all holy moments. (Don't let the word "holy" throw you. We'll circle back to it later.) For now, I want to encourage you to begin enlarging your idea of holiness, of what is sacred and what isn't. Forget the religious notions that come to mind when you hear the word and consider this instead: Every moment spent with God is holy because God is holy, and wherever we are, He is.

Breathe.

I've got fabulous news. Experiencing God in our everyday moments doesn't require us to live in a chapel or bunk down at the local church. We don't have to toss out our make-up and join a religious convent. We can perform any number of disciplines we consider spiritual and yet remain God-starved refugees if we don't learn how to engage God in between our devotionals and corporate services.

Heads up: Living the holy dare is full-throttle living, not boring, isolated inertia. We're about to peel away the religious rhetoric that so often surrounds the gift of Jesus, Immanuel, God with Us. Discovering all Jesus is in us may have us lifting our voices and yelling alongside a wise old prophet named Isaiah who once said:

Cry aloud and shout for joy, O inhabitant of Zion, For great in your midst is the Holy One of Israel (Isaiah 12:6 NASB).

Then again, it may not.

Knowledge alone won't blend our lives into one with His, and Truth that doesn't make it to our hearts becomes the dry root of religion.

But, hey, buckle up if you decide to take the holy dare of traveling with Jesus. Those who refuse to settle for anything less than He promised are in for one forevermore epic road trip!

What's Behind Your Happy Face?

Remember that "less-than" living I mentioned in the Introduction? This is what I'm talking about. We step just inside the door of faith, embrace a restored relationship with God through faith in Jesus, and then we go about acting like that's enough. Well, it's no longer enough for me. And since you're reading a book about finding the deep and wide life, I don't think it's enough for you either. Nor is it biblical.

Less-than living is a substandard Christian existence that doesn't bless the believer, and it'll never see the believer become a blessing to anyone else. But it doesn't have to be a permanent condition. God has secured for Himself a home in us forever, and He'll teach the willing how to share this new life together.

The Bible says we can learn to experience life with the One who gifts it, and I'm snapping-turtle stubborn about doing just that. I don't want to come one hair's width short of experiencing what I can of the mystery. The "hope of glory" lives in me.

To them God has chosen to make known among the Gentiles the glorious riches of this mystery, which is Christ in you, the hope of glory (Colossians 1:27 NIV).

I've become a squeaky wheel, asking God not to let me settle anywhere short of knowing Him as intimately as I can this side of Heaven. Jesus paid the ultimate cost to reconcile me to God. Like Paul, I want to lay hold of His purposes for laying hold of me.

Not that I have already obtained all this, or have already arrived at my goal, but I press on to take hold of that for which Christ Jesus took hold of me (Philippians 3:12 NIV).

I want you to locate that same desire within yourself. I know it's there because God put it there, and I intend to throw spiritual gas on it. The Scriptures are replete with God's desire to live with us and not just visit when we're feeling presentable. Tracing this divine longing will tantalize us with promise. So, too, will isolating the biographies of a few mortals who chose to take God up on His offer! Together, we'll see what we can learn from them, and we'll see how the God who fitted us for such relationship provided everything we need to experience it. We'll see how He leaves each of us the choice to embrace such a life or forfeit it. And before we're done, we'll look at ways to say yes to the promises!

The Great Divide Shouldn't Be

To understand God's priceless invitation and just how equipped we are to answer it, we'll need to start at the very beginning—and by that, I mean man's beginning. By way of reminder, Genesis isn't a record of the beginning of God. He has neither beginning nor end. Genesis opens with a record of God creating the world and proceeding to share Who He is by making man, in His own image, to dwell in it.

God knew the end from the beginning. He knew mankind would choose creation over the Creator and He'd have to pay the ultimate cost to redeem us—and still He brought us into existence, committed to rescuing us before we even needed rescue. Did we hear that? We often think of creation as God's first work. It wasn't. Redemption was. God's costly and perfect plan to give up His only begotten Son to give us eternal life was conceived before we were. The promise of redemption came before man's first breath.

For you know that it was not with perishable things such as silver or gold that you were redeemed from the empty way of life handed down to you from your ancestors, but with the precious blood of Christ, a lamb without blemish or defect. He was chosen before the creation of the world but was revealed in these last times for your sake (1 Peter 1:18-20 NIV).

Understanding this, let's look at the first glimpse of man. The beginning of the record of God and man opens with these words:

"Let Us make man in Our image, according to Our likeness." (Genesis 1:26 NASB)

Men and women much more educated and wiser than I line up all over the place as to what it means to be made in the image and likeness of God. Some say it refers to our physical nature. Others say it concerns our souls. Still others believe it refers to our spirits. May I suggest we combine all their theories? Not just our hearts, not just our spirits, and not just our natures are made in God's image, but the entirety of who we are and the whole of our human experience has been purposed to be able to receive His image and represent His likeness. We have eyes because He sees, ears because He hears, and thinking minds because He is wisdom.

Wild guess here, but I bet you didn't star that paragraph, underline it, or rush to share it on social media. That's okay for now, but I aim to convince you of just how life-changing that truth is before we're done.

Here's the thing, and it's a very big thing: Failing to understand we're each born to be physical imagers of an invisible God in every way—spirit, soul, and body—often keeps us from enjoying God's Presence outside what we consider more religious endeavors. It's a life-limiting secular/sacred mindset, and though we may never have put it in those words, it mires us in religious therapy sessions when our hungry hearts need a steady IV drip of Jesus. (Not clear on what I mean by that secular/sacred divide? Stay with me.)

Those same brilliant theological types have written volumes of works on this secular/sacred plague. This will surprise exactly no one who knows me, but "scholarly" misses me by a country mile—and that may be a good thing for our purposes. Let's break the concept down into everyman language.

The secular/sacred divide is our tendency to segment our days into holy times where we anticipate the possibility of experiencing God and common, everyday spaces where we don't think God wants an invite. Our thinking goes:

I'm at church. I expect to experience God here, so I'm reaching for Him.

I'm in line at the movies. I'm not expecting to experience God here, so I'm not looking for Him.

That's the secular/sacred mindset in a nutshell.

Oh, sure. We've heard the catchphrases from the latest bestsellers and big-time bloggers. They've told us driving a tractor can be a holy exercise and clearing the dishes can be a sacred moment, but it sounds like pied-piper music to our overly committed souls. Finding God in the laundry room? Communing while we commute? We'd love to believe such things were possible for Joe and Jane Believer and not just experiences reserved for God's Rock-Star Saints, but it sounds so unattainable, like we'd be living our lives with God instead of always trying to carve out time for Him in the daily chaos. Could such supernatural living really be possible?

Yes, it could. And yes, it is.

In my book *Heart Wide Open*, I wrote that God wants out of our quiet times and into our timelines, meaning out of the borders of our devotionals and into the rest of our day. Perhaps you're thinking, *That sounds like a fine idea, Shellie. But kind of unrealistic without the monastery move you mentioned earlier.* Granted, none of us would dare voice such thoughts lest we lose our reserved seating at the religious table with the super-spiritual people. (I only know these things because I've thought them.)

But not only is it possible; it's the very life God promised.

Let's jump into Genesis and see what's available on the holy page. The natural ease of life, human hand clasped in divine hand, is witnessed in man's first home with God—and this Garden of Eden version of life with God was all His idea.

All. His. Idea. Let that sink in and meet me in the next chapter.

Questions for Group Study or Private Reflection

1. Why can't God's plan to save us be separated from His desire to walk through this life with us?

2. Shellie describes the Big Lie as our tendency to hold onto some measure of independence from God in our quest for the fullest, most satisfying life. Can you identify with that? Why or why not?
3. Define the secular/sacred divide in your own words.

Chapter Three

. . . . .

Wake Up Little Suzy, Wake Up

*"The Gospel is not how people get to heaven.
The Gospel is how people get to God."*

—JOHN PIPER

My son is a hard worker—and a heavy sleeper. I remember trying to get him up for school. Teenage Phillip had a way of pretending to be fully conscious while he was still semi-sleeping, so I'd leave the room before I completely woke him from his early-morning coma. As frustrating as I found it to rouse Phillip back in the day, it became just as funny when his darling wife inherited the task.

Carey was great with child when she admitted she was hoping to go into labor during the day, when Phillip was his competent, coherent self. Apparently, the young couple had experienced something of a trial run when their horse got out of the pasture in the dark of night, and the resulting adventure didn't bode well for middle-of-the-night hospital runs. Carey said Phillip's eyes were open during the great horse escape and he was trying his best to communicate, but it was obvious to his pregnant wife that he was not really present. He might be home, technically speaking, but the blinds were still drawn.

I need to clarify. Phillip has since learned to wake at full steam, but I can relate to his earlier problems. I'm a light sleeper most of the time, but all bets are off if I allow myself the luxury of a Sunday afternoon nap. A Sunday nap renders me unconscious. We're talking *drool sleeping*. Waking up is insanely difficult, and once I do manage to come to the land of the living, it still takes a good bit of time before I'm fully functioning.

In some ways, our new birth in Christ is like that. We've come alive to God's presence, but our faculties and senses need a ton of renewing. The Bible even uses the imagery of sleepwalking to bid us deeper into a life shared with Christ.

For this reason it says, "Awake, sleeper, and arise from the dead, and Christ will shine on you." (Ephesians 5:14 NASB)

Indeed, the Bible describes us as sleeping and dead to all that is holy before we come to Christ. But once He brings us to life through faith in Jesus, this God of ours wants us to know life as we were meant to live it. It's as if He says, "Wake up, child. I have things to show you!" Consider how ridiculous we are to respond with an attitude that says something like, "Well, I can do Sundays and maybe a couple mornings a week, but time is money and the to-do list is long. It'll have to be quick. Chop-chop, God."

Irrational? Yes. But equally foolish and even sadder is the kind of religious response I've already admitted to having had at one point in my life. Like Mercy, the rescue dog, our actions say, "I'm really just here for the eternal security clause."

Silly us. Like Phillip trying to pretend to be awake so he could keep sleeping, if we try to grasp this new life in Christ while clinging to what we think of as our "real lives," it's to our great loss. If we try to hold Christ with one hand and our independent pursuits of what we think will fulfill us and make us happy in the other, we're doomed to stumble along semi-asleep, missing the promise of Jesus, God with us.

Do you want to wake up to everything God desires out of this friendship that cost Him so dearly? I do! I'm tired of dozing in semi-awareness of what God has done through Christ. I want to be fully alive in Him and help others live. I don't want to sleepwalk through the motions of this life in some vague hope of what waits in the next. (Later we'll talk about how finding the deep and wide life equips us to become a life-giving source for our friends and family!)

For now, there's a choice on the table. A most blessed choice. We can acknowledge that our senses are still dull and fuzzy. We can face the truth. Our sleepy spiritual eyes need training to focus on anything beyond our smart phones, and our dull spiritual ears need to learn how to listen for Him above the noise of our notifications.

If I were you, I'd be thinking, *I'm going to need chocolate and coffee. Lots of chocolate and coffee because this sounds strenuous.* And then I'd be thinking, *I get your theory, but how am I supposed to do this? How can I go from deaf to God to hearing Him speak, from blind to God's work to recognizing His ways?*

The foot-stomping good news? We aren't left here to wander around on our own after our long nap, running our toes into the spiritual furniture at every turn. God wants to do this thing with us! It's Follow the Leader, Jesus style.

By way of reminder, our goal for looking into the Garden story is seeing how God has always desired to be involved in our lives and how uniquely designed we are to enjoy His company. So, back to good old Adam. Let's see what we can learn about his arrival on planet Earth.

Life from the Get-Go

The LORD God planted a garden toward the east, in Eden; and there He placed the man whom He had formed (Genesis 2:8 NASB).

The man was created and placed in God's garden. We need to savor that. Man was placed, put, and positioned in God's delightful garden. He was chosen to receive His Maker's favor though he had not done a single religiousy thing to earn it. (You won't find "religiousy" in the dictionary. I made it up, and I define it as any action undertaken to atone for one's mistakes, get God's attention, or earn His favor.)

Through no merit of his own, Adam was admitted into the existing fellowship of God the Father, God the Son, and God the Holy Spirit. God said, "Let Us" make man.

As the narrative unfolds, we're treated to scenes depicting the Creator's ongoing desire to be present with man, enjoying the gift of life with him. That's tantalizing by itself, but what we don't see is also intriguing: We aren't given a picture of Adam in a futile search for a distant Creator.

Instead, we see Adam gifted with God's company and friendship from the get-go. Creator and creation know each other and enjoy each other, walk together and talk together. Their communication was easy and unhindered. The Bible even records God parading the animals past Adam to let him name them.

Out of the ground the Lord God formed every beast of the field and every bird of the sky, and brought them to the man to see what he would call them; and whatever the man called a living creature, that was its name (Genesis 2:19 NASB).

You know what else we don't see? Adam trying to find time for God. Not a hint of "Yeah, so I'd like to stay and chat, God, but I have animals to name and a garden to keep."

Adam's life before the Fall was marked by easy companionship with God. That bears zero similarity to my past religious experience. Zero, as in none. Nada.

Charting my spiritual progress by my spiritual performance didn't produce anything close to such a heavenly relationship. But I'll tell you what has: Daring to believe I'm as loved and accepted by God as He says I am and finding that He is the satisfaction I'm guilty of trying to find on my own. This is changing everything. And every tiny morsel of life with Him leaves me wanting more. I aim to find Him in every happy, sad, painful, pleasurable, frustrating, satisfying, relaxing, so-busy-I-can't-see-straight moment, because He has taught me that He truly is found by those who seek Him.

But we all know that seeking verse, right? *And if you seek Him, He will let you find Him* (2 Chronicles 15:2 NASB). So why do we continue to live at a distance? That's a very big why. I'll throw out more than one answer before we're done, and my list will be far from definitive. But it will be a starting place for anyone wanting to find a deep and wide life with God this side of Heaven.

Breathing Never Felt So Good

One of the reasons we live at a distance from God is rooted in the secular/sacred mentality we've already mentioned. It's our unspoken misunderstanding that God built shallow activities like eating, drinking, waking, and sleeping in our lives as filler around our holier moments when our oh-so-common activities are as potentially sacred as Easter Sunday. When lived with God and before God, all of life is sacred—by design. And when God is intentionally enthroned and worshipped in our daily lives, everything becomes holy.

Jesus made this promise of divine companionship to those who trusted in Him. *After a little while the world will no longer see Me, but you will see Me; because I live, you will live also. In that day you will know that I am in My Father, and you in Me, and I in you* (John 14:19-20 NASB).

Refusing to settle for anything less than that will cause us to live always breaking camp to follow Jesus around the next bend. It entices us to find more ways to share our lives with the Lover of our Souls! It's a mysterious reality. You and I have been given access through Jesus Christ to experience a life in which we are spiritually seated with

Him in heavenly places, even as we walk in this world among fellow mortals in one of our big-box stores buying paper towels. Our challenge lies in learning how to live up to our privileges.

Thankfully, God knew we'd need continuing education. We've been given His Holy Spirit as our teacher and the Bible as our textbook.

And do not be conformed to this world, but be transformed by the renewing of your mind, so that you may prove what the will of God is, that which is good and acceptable and perfect (Romans 12:2 NASB).

Perfection isn't expected in this course, but attendance is vital. Without it, we'll spend the rest of our days here like sleepy Shellie after a Sunday afternoon nap, living our new life in Christ like the lights are on but nobody's home.

There's a lot more to be learned from the Garden story about precisely how fitted we are for a life few dare to live. Some would even say it's as easy as breathing, but then, we humans are good at making the simple serious. How about a story for illustration?

My high school cheerleader suit hangs in the back of my cedar closet to this day. It's like I expect my old high school to call one day with an emergency. *"Shellie!" a breathless voice will yell into the phone. "We're short a cheerleader! We need you to get your uniform and get here as quickly as you can!"* You're right, and I am weird, but there's a story on the table.

My sister Rhonda was on that same cheer squad. One fall afternoon, yours truly and another cheerleader were trying to help Rhonda learn a new stunt during practice. The process was simple. The results became serious faster than quick.

Rhonda was supposed to run toward me and our friend, Ruby. The two of us were facing Rhonda with our hands in front of us, knees bent, fingers intertwined. The idea was for Rhonda to run toward us, jump into the air, and land with one foot in Ruby's hands and one in mine, all so we could help her spring up high enough to tuck, backflip, and land on her feet.

Tucking was important. Rhonda didn't tuck well.

I remember her sailing backwards in slow motion. Picture the arc of a rainbow and you'll see it, too. Rhonda's maiden voyage ended in a crash and burn situation with her lying on the ground and the rest of us screaming like, well, like teenage girls. *"Breathe! Breathe, Rhonda!"*

Ruby may have been the least helpful. Not because she didn't care. Ruby cared plenty! But in her excitement, she got her words twisted. The rest of us were torn between helping Rhonda survive and trying not to bust a gut as Ruby implored my traumatized sister to *"Deathe breeply!"*

Thankfully, Rhonda was able to breathe deeply soon enough, despite our well-meaning but inadequate assistance. I'm about to take a similarly excited stab at how God fashioned us to enjoy Him. My expertise will fall probably as short as our high school medical advice, but it won't be dangerous, so there's that.

You Were Made for This

Understanding God literally fashioned us to enjoy Him is as crucially important to our God-hungry souls as the next breath of air is to our physical bodies. According to the Word, the breath of God Himself was in Adam's nostrils. *Then the Lord God formed man of dust from the ground, and breathed into his nostrils the breath of life; and man became a living being* (Genesis 2:7 NASB).

Is it in us? Yes! *Who among all these does not know That the hand of the Lord has done this, In whose hand is the life of every living thing, And the breath of all mankind?* (Job 12:9-10 NASB)

Confirmation. We have the breath of God in our lungs, just like Adam! *Okay*, you might say, *but according to the Bible, so do cows and ladybugs.*

If He put His mind to it and withdrew the spirit and breath He gave, every living thing would perish together ... (Job 34:14-15 HCSB)

Correct, but there's an important difference between humans having God's breath in our lungs and other living things being dependent on that same breath. Cows and ladybugs don't bear His image. We do! And this image is our invitation to enjoy His company. Mankind alone was meant to know Him, by design.

Let's look at it this way: The appliances in our homes are powered by electricity. When we switch on a lamp, an electrical current causes it to glow. Electricity also powers a lot of other things in our homes, but only those with a receptacle (bulb) capable of receiving the circuit have the potential to shine. (A night-light has this potential; a blender does not.)

In the same way, every living thing receives breath from God, but humans alone are built to receive that breath in a custom-made way that provides for relationship. We alone are fashioned in His image, and this is our receptacle for experiencing God. From the beginning, God knew us and created us with an ability to know Him.

May we never settle for anything less than the full potential of our design. God wants to walk through all of life with us, the marvelous and the messy, the holy and the hellacious.

Having established that God designed Adam (and likewise us) to know Him, let's keep reading.

Then the Lord God took the man and put him into the garden of Eden to cultivate it and keep it. The Lord God commanded the man, saying, "From any tree of the garden you may eat freely; but from the tree of the knowledge of good and evil you shall not eat, for in the day that you eat from it you will surely die." (Genesis 2:15-17 NASB)

We all know what's coming, don't we? We're looking at the potential danger that comes with being made in God's image. With Adam's extravagant birthright came the autonomy God Himself enjoyed, a free will. And this great and powerful gift of choice? Again, all God's idea.

God knew the potential danger inherent in the free will He gave this new creation. He spelled out in the clearest terms both the promise and the pitfall that came with it. What His crowning creation chose to do with this great gift of choice would determine whether they would enjoy the incomprehensible blessing of knowing life in God's presence or forfeit it.

It still does.

Deathe breeply, y'all.

Questions for Group Study or Private Reflection

1. How does the Bible characterize Adam's earliest relationship with God in the Garden? And how does that compare to your faith walk?
2. Can you explain what you think Shellie means by "charting her spiritual progress"? Have you ever done that?
3. In Shellie's electrical appliance analogy, what is our "receptable" that sets us apart and makes us capable of knowing God?

Chapter Four

·····

A Forfeit Is a Forfeit is a Forfeit

*"In a nutshell, the Bible from Genesis 2 to Revelations 22
tells the story of a God reckless with desire to get His family back."*

—PHILLIP YANCEY

As a little girl growing up on the end of a Louisiana dirt path known as Bull Run Road, few things excited me more than having a slumber party with friends, especially during the long months of summer vacation. This can be attributed to the narrowness of my social circle when school was out of session.

Living in the country often limited Shellie Charlene's playmates to my two older sisters, Cynthia Darlene and Rhonda Arlene. My enthusiasm for overnight company whose names didn't rhyme with my own often caused me to lose my young mind and plead with my parents to let a friend stay overnight even as the potential guest stood there looking hopeful. Bad move on Shellie Charlene's part. Really bad move. Begging for a playdate was frowned on in our house, but doing so in front of the potential date was far worse. It put Mama in a bad spot and me in a dangerous one!

I can still hear her saying, "If you know what's good for you, you'll stop right there. You're about to get more than you bargained for!"

This was Mama's way of suggesting I consider the consequences of my behavior while I still could. To "get more than you bargained for" was one of her go-to expressions, and the implication was the surprise wouldn't be pleasant. I'm not sure a better example of this adage exists than what we find in the Garden of Eden when man first rebelled against his Maker.

There's no scriptural evidence Adam or Eve set out to create distance between themselves and God when they took of the forbidden fruit. Scripture records Eve's thought process prior to The Big Bite, and nowhere in it do we see her expressing a desire to forfeit the relationship she enjoyed with God!

Then the woman saw that the tree was good for food and delightful to look at, and that it was desirable for obtaining wisdom. So she took some of its fruit and ate it; she also gave some to her husband, who was with her, and he ate it (Genesis 3:6 HCSB).

Eve simply decided she was the best judge of what she needed. She reserved the right to decide what was the most desirable and beautiful and what she needed to be wise. She chose to ignore God's warning to pursue her conclusions.

Consider the wisdom part of the equation for a moment. Have you ever wondered who Eve intended to impress with her new smarts? Her social circle included God and Adam. It's not like she could use her new and improved intuition to question her man's sincerity when he said, "Eve, darling, you're the only woman in the world for me." I mean, she *was* the only woman in the world! You don't need to outshine human competition when you don't have any. I think it's safe to say Eve wasn't planning to amaze God with her brilliance. That leaves one person: Eve herself. Eve's fruit fascination sprang from the secret desires of her own heart.

The prospect of gaining wisdom speaks the language of achievement and acknowledgement. Affirmation stoked Eve's pride, and it stokes ours. (Anyone else thinking of social "shares," "follows," and "likes"?) Eve's conclusion that the fruit was attractive, tasty, and promised her wisdom presented her with all the appeals of the world around us. She bought into the devil's persuasion: *There is something more and better out there than God is offering.* This is the lie Eve embraced that set her up for the Fall.

Heads up, friend: Eve's enemy is ours, and he still peddles the same old poison! He tries to sell us the same lie he sold Eve, that surrendering our liberty limits our fulfillment, when the opposite is true. To lose self is to gain Christ, and He is everything. But God's adversary never stops trying to convince us a better, more exciting, more rewarding, more restful, more promising, more fulfilling life can be found outside of God—and he never stops encouraging us to exercise our presumed right to pursue our "best life."

I know this one, y'all. I'm forever grateful for God's incredible patience with me back when I thought I needed space for me as much, if not more, than I needed Him. Too honest? Wince if you must, but please keep reading. Never would I have said it aloud (as if that means God wouldn't know), but I once had thoughts that went something like this: *All right, already! I believe in Jesus, but does my whole life have to revolve around Him? What about* me?

If I could go back in time and address that version of me, I would tell her what I've discovered. The greatest life, the fullest life, that best life I thought I was after, is the life in which God is always enthroned and never "set aside," whether I'm sitting in a church service or tubing on the lake.

Jesus is eternal life, and He is here. When living in awareness of Him becomes our goal, He nourishes our souls out of that pursuit, and He reshapes us into who He made us to be, one moment at a time.

Like this one.

I'm aware of Jesus now, though my fingers are busy typing and my mind is choosing one word over a dozen others as I listen to one of my labs snoring at my feet and watch his brother chasing a squirrel. My iPhone is beeping with messages, and I can feel the breeze from the porch fans stirring the humid air of this warm Louisiana day. *I am not consciously praying, and yet I'm aware of Him, and this awareness is Life.*

Turns out, my independent pursuit of what I thought I needed was keeping me from everything I wanted. Who knew? God. It's why He demands we love Him with our whole heart, mind, and strength because wholehearted loving is the life that learns to enjoy Him, and the life that comes to enjoy Him and treasure Him as highest and best *is our best life.*

This is my story, and it is much like Eve's. We can learn a lot about ourselves from her. For now, I want to zero in on the tragic consequence of the first couple's mutual decision to pursue their own will over God's.

Giving Up Glory

That decision created a great gulf between God and man where there had previously been sweet friendship and ongoing conversation. Think about what that meant. Eve could've raised her children in the Garden of Eden. She could've kissed their baby toes and watched them learn to walk in Paradise. Had she not bought the lie that God was holding out on them, she could've continued to enjoy those afternoon walks with her Creator, her man, and her babies. *Eve could've tended to her little ones' needs even as God tended to hers.* As it was, the unlimited possibilities of divine relationship and all it offered for her present and her future were traded off for a mirage promising more.

Eve is us. We remain susceptible to her fatal mistake of looking around God to reach for His creation. This is how Genesis records God's response to the couple's fateful choice, because of course you know Adam followed suit.

Then the LORD *God said, "Behold, the man has become like one of Us, knowing good and evil; and now, he might stretch out his hand, and take also from the tree of life, and eat, and live forever"—therefore the Lord God sent him out from the garden of Eden, to cultivate the ground from which he was taken. So He drove the man out; and at the east of the garden of Eden He stationed the cherubim and the flaming sword which turned every direction to guard the way to the tree of life* (Genesis 3:22-24 NASB).

If this were a reality television show, I'd be tempted to change the channel. I don't enjoy watching other people's misery disguised as entertainment. (There's nothing real about twenty men wooing one woman with dinner and roses while each one hopes he'll make the next cut in her search for Mr. Right. And there's nothing entertaining about watching people eat disgusting things like boiled snake and live hissing cockroaches. But I digress.)

Life doesn't get more real than what happened at the Fall. As tempting as it might be to lower our eyes and rush past this woeful scene when our first parents had to leave the Garden, it'd be a grave mistake. There's far too much to learn. For example, we're told God sent man out of the Garden, and in the next breath, we're told He drove the fallen couple out. Sent them out and drove them out is an interesting progression. Does it mean anything?

Let's look closer.

Perhaps with a bit of imagination, we can envision some of the drama hinted at here. (If we don't make a new doctrine out of our discussion, we won't be guilty of violating the Scriptures.) Imagining what it was like at the scene will help us get into the story.

While Eve and then Adam weighed the cost of eating from the banned tree and decided it was worth the risk, the couple had now come to the moment of reckoning. The promise of death they'd dismissed in the moment of temptation was now exploding in full color, and their first vivid illustration of this experience called death was seeing God slay an animal to clothe their shame.

I write to you from the deep South, where I've lived my entire life. I've seen deer skinned, chickens plucked, and fish cleaned from the time I was old enough to wrinkle my nose and look away. (For educational purposes, a chicken really can run around with its head cut off, at least temporarily.) My point? Witnessing God slaying those animals for their hides wouldn't have been enjoyable for me, but it wouldn't have rocked my world. This, however, wasn't playing out before the eyes of a country girl on a rural farm in the Louisiana Delta. This was Eden. Can I remind you that nothing similar had ever happened in Paradise? Neither human nor animal had died even the most peaceful death, and this demise was anything but serene. This dramatic dying was awash in fresh, red blood.

In case you're wondering, we're not told if Adam and Eve witnessed the animal's death. We don't know if the sounds and smells of death were assaulting their senses and tearing at their raw emotions. Even if they didn't see the animal being slain and its lifeblood slipping away, they were in the middle of a staggering new experience as freshly removed animal skins are wrapped around their naked bodies. Those smelly skins were bringing overpowering sensory evidence. Death has indeed entered their perfect world—as promised.

For what it's worth, I lean toward thinking Adam and Eve witnessed the slaying of their substitute. I don't believe the sacrifice was handled off-scene and out of sight because the animal's death in the Garden that day foreshadowed the crucifixion of Heaven's perfect Lamb, and history records friend and foe witnessing that awful sacrifice.

They were experiencing the brutal results wrapped around their bodies, and the worst lay straight ahead. As horrid as the entrance of physical death must have been for the fallen couple, Adam and Even were facing something immeasurably more devastating: spiritual death. They were being banished from God's intimacy, and neither Adam nor Eve had ever known life apart from friendship with God. From the very first moment Adam opened his eyes, He had known God's presence. The first time Eve stood, it was before her Maker.

Could it get any worse? Yes, it could. And yes, it did.

In addition to witnessing their first physical death and facing the ugly reality of spiritual death and the incomparable loss of God's company, the couple now realized it was all going to happen somewhere … out … there … beyond Eden.

They were going to experience death alone one day, somewhere beyond the security of their glorious garden, separated from their God. They forfeited the single greatest promise of their existence: Enjoying life with the One who gave, protected, and nourished it in the sanctuary of His company.

I wish we could go to video here. Were the broken pair pleading with God over His pronouncement that it was time for them to leave the garden, or were they stunned into silence? I would've been begging Him for mercy, for one more chance to do it right.

If they were pleading, perhaps their cries are behind that progression I noted earlier. Remember when we read God "sent them out" before we read that He "drove them out"? Maybe there's no significance to the slight difference in phrasing. But maybe there is.

As we continue to let our imaginations explore this tragic scene, please remember we're not making a doctrinal point. We're using our God-given imaginations to put ourselves in the moment. That said, look over there, beneath the tree.

There's Eve, and she's weeping in the heaving, gut-wrenching way that suggests her heart is breaking in a thousand pieces. See Adam's tear-stained face as he puts his arm around her shaking shoulders. He's clenching his jaw the way my man does when tragedy strikes our family, when he's burdened by his own pain but suffering even more under the weight of mine. Did Adam and Eve's eyes meet in shame before their gazes raced back to God in panic? We don't know. We don't know if they whined, begged, and pleaded to stay with God in the Garden. We do know Paradise was sealed right along with their fate when they chose their will over God's. Genesis describes what happened next.

So He drove the man out; and at the east of the garden of Eden He stationed the cherubim and the flaming sword which turned every direction to guard the way to the tree of life (Genesis 3:24 NASB).

Not just banished.

Banned.

This was their "more than they bargained for" moment.

I'll never believe that being banished from the presence of God was a conscious choice Adam or Eve made. You simply can't convince me they understood by choosing to do life their way, they were cutting themselves off from His.

We never do.

They simply chose to believe they were the best judges of what they needed to live their best life, to borrow that trendy phrase, and in doing so, they forfeited the privilege of knowing God. Their choice brought death because it separated them from Life.

It still does.

You and I forfeit intimacy with God every time we swallow the lie that we can find more of what we need outside of Him than we can with and through Him. Think back to Mercy the Refugee and how his wariness reminded me of my own history with God. Remember my uncomfortable confession about wanting to hold onto the life He was offering with one hand—if I could retain some measure of *me* where I could pursue my own agenda with the other? I can still do that. Today. The author writing the words you're reading. How's that for transparency?

Oh, I've fallen hard for Jesus. He has long since moved from being a side dish on my crowded plate to becoming both my full meal and delicious dessert. I now live convinced He is the life I crave. And yet . . . because I live in this body, in this realm, I can still be tempted on any given day to believe I know what I need for the mood I'm in or the circumstances I'm facing, and I can still entertain the enemy's suggestion that the answer can be found apart from Jesus.

Sometimes I'm slower to recognize the lie than at other times, but at least I'm on guard now and I know where to go for reinforcements. Like the great Apostle Paul, I've discovered the power in confessing what God already knows: Left to my own, my heart reaches for the wrong fix every time. But I'm not on my own—and neither are you, and as we'll see as we move through Scripture, neither was the apostle Paul. His strength was owning his need for Jesus.

Paul owned the problem of having a heart that tripped him up despite his best intentions, but he also knew victory was found in Jesus, the heart-fixer. Paul celebrated this victory at the end of his better-known confession, but we often stop before we get to his hallelujah party. We leave Paul dangling, complaining that he couldn't do what he wanted to do and admitting he did what he didn't want to do, and we use his words as an excuse for staying in our mess. *Why, even Paul said he did what he didn't want to do ...*

We owe the man an apology. Paul wasn't saying all is lost; he was saying all is won! Follow me to the next chapter, and I'll show you what I mean.

Questions for Group Study or Private Reflection

1. The devil convinced Eve that surrendering her liberty limited her _____.
2. Shellie paints a bloody picture of the consequences of the Fall. What animal do you think may have been slain to make their coverings, and what makes you think so? The Bible doesn't tell us, so there is no wrong answer.
3. Can you identify something you repeatedly do that you don't want to do?

Chapter Five

. . . . .

When You're All Out of Sync

> *"I have heard of some good old woman in a cottage,*
> *who had nothing but a piece of bread and a little water.*
> *Lifting up her hands, she said as a blessing,*
> *'What! All this, and Christ too?'"*
>
> —CHARLES SPURGEON

Last summer, I made some substantial changes here at All Things Southern. For starters, I moved from hosting my radio program live from a nearby station to podcasting from my home here on the banks of Lake Providence, Louisiana. Although I've been in radio for almost two decades, podcasting has come with its own learning curve. File it under "old dog, new trick."

For instance, my radio audience had been accustomed to me going Facebook live during the radio show. I wanted to try to recapture some of that for them because they've always been so loyal. Now, *why* they've been so loyal—that's a mystery. I've never hosted your average radio show. I chat about whatever comes up in my head, which can be fun or scary—or both—and I interview interesting people. But, to my point, I set up a camera to capture some video while my podcasting equipment was recording the audio.

I wrapped, thinking, *That went well.* Wrong. The video was sailing around Facebook before I realized what I was saying was all out of sync with what I was doing, and I'd been too busy recording my efforts to notice. That's nothing more than a social media fail, but it's sobering in the way it mirrors my Christian experience.

I hadn't been pursuing Jesus long before I realized how challenging it was to sync my talk with my walk. (Can I get an amen? A whisper will do.)

Thankfully, I've made the same discovery as the Apostle Paul. God has made it possible for the way we want to live for Jesus to sync with what we say we believe about Jesus. Let's head to the seventh chapter of Romans, where Paul lays out the problem.

For the good that I want, I do not do, but I practice the very evil that I do not want. But if I am doing the very thing I do not want, I am no longer the one doing it, but sin which dwells in me. I find then the principle that evil is present in me, the one who wants to do good. For I joyfully concur with the law of God in the inner man, but I see a different law in the members of my body, waging war against the law of my mind and making me a prisoner of the law of sin which is in my members (Romans 7:19-23 NASB).

Following this admission about his broken want-to, Paul begs a question: *Wretched man that I am! Who will set me free from the body of this death?* (Romans 7:24 NASB)

Paul wasn't asking because he was doomed with no hope of changing! His was a rhetorical question, and the man couldn't answer himself fast enough in verse 25 when he shouted, *"Thanks be to God through Jesus Christ our Lord!"* Okay, I can't prove he was shouting, but I think he was. And not because my translation has an exclamation point following his celebration but because I'm learning the joy of his discovery.

In the same breath Paul uses to bemoan his powerlessness against the sin warring in his want-to, the grateful apostle shares the exciting discovery of his new life in Christ, and his testimony can be and is *meant* to be ours. Sin's stranglehold dies when we yield to the Spirit of Jesus, Who lives in us and with us.

Paul had discovered Jesus was living in Him to heal the weakness of his old nature, and he was therefore no longer condemned to it. As Paul says, "The law of the Spirit of life in Christ Jesus has set you free from the law of sin and death!"

This victory extends to you and me. The Spirit of the victorious Christ in us can reign over our broken nature. When our heart is cold and we're tempted to reach for creation instead of our Creator, we can run to Him for help. We can tell Him we want to want Him more than we do the temporary fixes around us, and we can ask Him to heal our divided hearts, again, and help us hunger for Him, again. The Healer never tires of healing. I'm forever asking Jesus to alert me when I'm falling for the lie, and I find Him beyond faithful to answer!

So, yes, this is me, admitting I've often stood beside Eve, participating in a fallen moment. And, forgive me for getting in your business, but I suspect you've stood there with us a time or ten thousand yourself. (Maybe you're standing there now.)

As it turns out, our bid for finding fulfillment independent of God is as old as the Garden of Eden. So let's delve back into Eve's story, which will help us learn to avoid the enemy's age-old but ever-present traps meant to distance us from God's Presence.

The third chapter of Genesis opens with the description of the devil, in his craftiness, approaching the woman with what seems to be a harmless question.

Now the serpent was more crafty than any beast of the field which the LORD *God had made. And he said to the woman, "Indeed, has God said, 'You shall not eat from any tree of the garden'?"*

The woman said to the serpent, "From the fruit of the trees of the garden we may eat; but from the fruit of the tree which is in the middle of the garden, God has said, 'You shall not eat from it or touch it, or you will die.'"

The serpent said to the woman, "You surely will not die! For God knows that in the day you eat from it your eyes will be opened, and you will be like God, knowing good and evil." (Genesis 3:1-5 NASB)

Freeze. Since we all know Eve eats the apple, let's push pause to make a couple of crucial observations. When initially questioned about their preapproved menu by the devil, (masquerading as a snake), Eve says she and Adam are allowed to eat from all the trees except the one in the middle of the garden. So far, so good. But, then, in verse 3, Eve elaborates, adding that they aren't allowed to even *touch* that forbidden tree! Wait. What? God's original command didn't include a no-touch rule. Could Eve's ad lib mean she was chaffing at the restriction around the tree in the center of the garden? If so, it'd explain her willingness to listen to the devil's accusations. It may be his claims mirrored the suspicions she was already harboring: *God was too demanding. What good reason could there be for banning the fruit of this tree?*

Reader, beware. Writer, beware. If you have raised a child, know a child, or were ever a child (gotcha!), you know we're all born bristling against boundaries. We come here wanting our way. That attitude doesn't have to be taught, but it also does not have to define us. Grace can trump our nature. God has made a way for us to grow in our preference for His ways over our own.

The second warning we can take from Eve's conversation with the devil is that *she had a conversation with the devil.* Nothing good comes through dialoguing with the enemy about whether God has our best interests at heart. There's a reason Ephesians 4:27 tells us not to give the devil an opportunity: We won't act on doubts we refuse to entertain.

I was reading through this passage one day when I had the most sobering realization. This woman who was susceptible to the enemy's lies and fell for his insidious temptation was a woman who *walked and talked with God.* Whoa. That means Eve chose wrong after experiencing all that is right, and that's a flashing neon warning with my name on it. If Eve could do that, I can. You can, too.

When the woman saw that the tree was good for food, and that it was a delight to the eyes, and that the tree was desirable to make one wise, she took from its fruit and ate; and she gave also to her husband with her, and he ate (Genesis 3:6 NASB).

An apple is unlikely to be our downfall, but make no mistake, the core of Eve's temptation is ours (see what I did there?). The enemy bombards us with opportunities to draw conclusions that mirror hers. His strategy never changes. He never stops suggesting obeying God means missing out on the best this world has to offer. The devil wants us to believe God is holding out on us and we have the right to pursue what's behind Door Number Two, or Three, or Four ... He wins, too, unless we're intentional about looking to Jesus to satisfy our ever-hungry souls. Left to our own impulses, we'll choose wrong by default, and we'll sound much like Eve, thinking, *Hmmm ... that looks good, and that other one over there is attractive, and this thing here will make me wise. I need this, that, and the other to have the fullest life, to live my best life. Why can't I just reach out and take it?*

Because it's all lies. Because temporary hits can't satisfy eternal hunger. Because whatever we reach for to make ourselves feel better today will become a fix we'll need more of tomorrow.

No amount of acquisitions, affirmations, or acclamations from creation can substitute for the Creator. We were created for God, and living for ourselves will always leave us empty. Jesus is the One we're longing for, and life is found in taking our cavernous souls to Him for filling.

With Jesus, there are no diminishing returns—just divine, compelling answers to our deepest desires to know and be known. He satiates our soul while stirring our longing. In Him, we find contentment laced with longing, satisfaction colored with the sweetest hunger. Strange? Yes. Otherworldly? Yes. That's Jesus. Ever-increasing joy and satisfaction lie in Jesus because in Him we taste the first course of eternity.

We'll return to Eden one more time in the pages ahead to talk about the privilege you and I have to reclaim our "fallen" moments and the choices that change everything. But for now, let's note the last line of Genesis 3:6. The Word tells us Eve took what she had just fed on and gave it to her husband. Oh, that this would sink deep into our hearts!

What you and I feed on can reshape our homes and our families— or destroy them. As surely as Eve passed the forbidden fruit on to her mate, you and I will pass on to our loved ones whatever we rely on to nourish ourselves, be that Christ or the empty promises around us.

Adam and Eve forfeited their intimacy with God by acting as their own final authorities on what they needed to be truly fulfilled. The Fall boiled down to the inevitable and tragic consequence of this willful independence from God. It's a costly lesson, and we keep repeating it, generation after generation. Choosing to pursue their own agendas forced Adam and Eve to leave the refuge they shared with God, and it stripped them of the privilege of eating freely from the Tree of Life. No more feasting on Life itself? Talk about getting more than you bargained for! The first couple discovered they couldn't enjoy life with their Maker based on their own rules of engagement. Neither can you. Neither can I. God's ways aren't restrictive weights but life-giving tools.

For the love of God is this, that we obey His commandments; and His commandments are not burdensome. For whatever is born of God conquers the world (1 John 5:3-4a NASB).

Knowing God is our best life because knowing God *is* Life. Listen to how Jesus said it.

This is eternal life, that they may know You, the only true God, and Jesus Christ whom You have sent (John 17:3 NASB).

Those are the words God used many years ago to set me on a hunt to know Him beyond what I had learned in pews from preachers. I wrote about that season of my life in my book *Heart Wide Open*.

My starts and stops, trips and falls, could fill a few more books, but here's my experience: When we set out to know God, we run headlong into His desire to be known. God loves first and best. Believing *He* is wooing *us* changes everything. The determined seeker can never want more of God than He is willing to give of Himself. The love of God is immeasurable and inexhaustible, and He mines miracles out of messes.

Grace Wins the Day

Last summer, my husband and I hosted our darling grandchildren, known around here as The Fabulous Five. It was the second annual no-adults-allowed Pops and Keggie Kamp. Pops functions as the responsible person on the premises (because someone must) while I fall into the no adults allowed category.

"Keggie" is my grandmother name. Years ago, my nieces' and nephews' efforts to say "Aunt Shellie" sounded like "Aunt Keggie." It stuck with friends and family, and when the grands came along, they picked it up on cue. Much of what happens at Pops and Keggie Kamp is meant to stay at Pops and Keggie Kamp (at least where their parents are concerned), but one story comes to mind that bears repeating here.

Kamp is full of tubing on the lake, visits to the farm, fun in the sun, and late-night movies. We enjoy popcorn, treats, arts, crafts, and snuggles galore. But, above all, Kamp is about reinforcing the Gospel of Christ their parents are teaching our grands. And that's why the Fabulous Five and I were circled up on the hard pavement of the carport one afternoon with me holding two shiny red apples. I had found a great lesson online and was eager to share the message.

We began by comparing the apples and agreeing they looked basically the same, until I proceeded to lead by horrible example. I held up one apple, remarked about its ugly skin, and dropped it.

I picked the apple back up and passed it to the next child, encouraging her to also say something mean to or about the apple. The grands giggled nervously. It took some prompting for them to get over the strangeness of it all, but one by one they got into the act of spewing ugly at the innocent piece of fruit.

My plan was to let the meanness happen and then slice open both apples to compare them a second time. I knew the outside of the apples would look pretty much the same, but I was counting on the insides to tell a different story. The bruised and brown flesh of the mistreated apple, as compared to the sweet white meat of the first apple, would help to impress a valuable truth on all of us: We might not see the damage our words and actions cause others, but the wounds are there, on the inside. Good plan? I thought so, too, but three kids into the illustration, life happened.

It was Grant's turn, the oldest grandson, our gentle, sensitive music lover, a basketball-loving sportsman with a competitive streak as long as his Keggie's. (Yet another confession there.) Grant ragged on the apple as instructed, but instead of dropping it on the pavement, he drew back and threw it at our feet as hard as he could. Ever seen an apple explosion? We have. The fruit went everywhere, covering all of us in bruised apple flesh.

Grant was instantly contrite. His big brown eyes filled with tears as he looked around at our tainted and shocked circle. No one had escaped the carnage of his decision.

Did you hear that? No one.

My best-laid plans lay in as many pieces as the apple. Five pairs of eyes watched me for the next move. I did some prayer peddling (my name for silent 911 calls to Heaven) as we all picked up the apple pieces and I ran interference for Grant with the other grands, who were none too happy about him upsetting Keggie's lesson. Weston was a little too young to understand what was happening, but his big sisters' eyes were saucer-huge, and Connor was vocally reprimanding his older brother. Me? I was so focused on my plan and the big fail that I almost missed the new beauty of the moment. Thankfully, light began to dawn.

I told the grands over popcorn with extra butter (popcorn is a great fixer) that our apple fiasco wasn't going to ruin everyone's Kamp. Grant was sorry, and Grant was forgiven. I told them I learned that from God. He loves me, He forgives me, and He lets me start over all the time. And then He asks me to forgive others and let them start over when they mess up, too. The biblical word is "redemption," but we didn't use it that day. It wasn't necessary.

Love spoke louder, and that very redeeming love of God is about to shine in all its brilliance as we return to the Fall of Man. Punishment has come down, and banishment is imminent for Adam and Eve, but Love is going to rule the day with a hint of Grace to come.

Have you ever stopped to consider that tossing the disobedient pair out of His presence wasn't God's only option in that dreadful moment of judgment? He had given his kids everything, they basically said it wasn't enough. He could've acted out of white-hot anger alone when their choices ruined everything. He could've looked at that discarded and darkening piece of fruit and chosen to do away with His created beings on the spot. God could've wiped them out of His garden and off His planet. Instead, He forced Adam and Eve out of paradise and commissioned fearsome angels to bookend a mighty flaming sword and stand guard at the garden's entrance to keep them from returning and eating from the tree of Life. Banished and barred by a fiery sentry.

I wouldn't be surprised if you are thinking, *Scary angels and a fiery sword? You call that a picture of redeeming love? I'm not seeing it, Shellie.*

Grab a scrap of paper and print this next line out where you can see it today and tomorrow. Put it on your refrigerator. Write it with lipstick on your bathroom mirror. Do whatever you need to do to hold on to it.

Man's sin against God did not extinguish
God's love for man.

It never does.

So tell me. Have you taken some bad roads, made some poor choices? You're still ridiculously loved by God, as demonstrated through Christ Jesus. You haven't worn His great love out, either. Your calling remains as firm as ever. Ask for forgiveness, celebrate His grace, and get back in the race. He waits for you.

Questions for Group Study or Private Reflection

1. It should give all of us pause to realize Eve fell into the devil's trap even though she _____ and _____ with God.
2. Can you explain why Shellie says Eve's temptation is ours?
3. No doubt we've all experienced the cycle of asking God for forgiveness, and then asking again and again because we don't feel forgiven. How does that affect your relationship with Him?

Chapter Six

. . . . .

When Mercy Keeps Coming

"Our lives are fashioned by our choices.
First we make our choices. Then our choices make us."

—ANNE FRANK

I f you haven't been tweeting with me on Twitter, following me on Facebook, or exchanging pics on Instagram (and if you aren't, let's fix that! I love sharing life with my readers), you may not be aware that our fifth and perhaps final grandchild, Weston Phillip Tomlinson, was born on November 13, 2013. Considering the ginormous number of pictures of Weston the Wonder Boy I collected on my iPhone, I feel I showed remarkable initial restraint in those early days by posting only a dozen or so. Key phrasing there would be "initial restraint." My self-imposed picture-posting limit blew up as I fell deeper and deeper in love with our newest little guy.

In those first few weeks, my relationship with Weston was all one-sided, but experience told me a day was coming when baby boy would turn his little head when he heard my voice. I knew one day he would smile at me in recognition. And he did. Oh, happy day! As much as I loved staring at Weston from Day One, my joy exploded when he began to light up when he saw me.

Did you know our deepening relationship with Christ brings Him a similar joy? Listen to these words. Jesus said, *I am the good shepherd, and I know My own and My own know Me, even as the Father knows Me and I know the Father; and I lay down My life for the sheep* (John 10:14-15 NASB).

That's Jesus, crowing over the fact that His sheep know Him. I love thinking on this. Jesus, Son of God, wants us to know Him. Our pursuit of Him brings Him joy! He expects us to come to recognize His voice and His ways, and He enjoys it, much the way we get excited when our newborns learn to recognize us.

May it be our mutual goal to invite God into our days and spend so much time listening for Him that the slightest whisper of our Beloved would catch our ears and find us turning toward that familiar Voice. Jesus knows us, one and all. Let's be found pressing in until our Savior can say with great delight that we know Him, too! It's our birthright, but we'll need to be intentional to realize it.

A life typified by perpetual companionship with God is available to all of us, but like Adam and Eve, we're prone to looking around God for what we think we need unless we choose to fix our eyes on Jesus and draw from Life Himself. In Him, we learn to choose. Without Him, we're perennially choice-challenged and headed for the dreadful consequences of our decisions.

Back to the Garden.

Have you ever told your children you didn't enjoy punishing them but it was for their own good? My sisters and I rued those words from our parents' lips, but years later, I found myself using similar lines with my kids, and surprise, surprise, I meant it. Multiply our human capacity to love our littles by infinity, and we'll get an inkling of what God was feeling when He banished the first couple from Eden. God's mighty love wouldn't let Him cast man off forever, but He loved them too much to let them stay. Why? Because the devil had sold the couple a half-truth. Twisted truth is his calling card.

Adam and Eve had indeed become like God in that they now knew good and evil. However, unlike their Creator, they had just presented irrefutable evidence that they were incapable of choosing the good! Had they eaten from the Tree of Life, mankind would have lived forever in their new state, shamed, choice-challenged, and separated from the Lover of their souls. God's great big heart couldn't permit it. I'm hoping every choice-challenged soul reading these words will join the choice-challenged soul writing them in sounding a grateful "Amen!"

There's misery washing over this scene, and there's sore judgment being handed down as the promised result of sin, but mercy is reigning. Why? Because the garden is sealed and the couple banned, but they aren't being cast away forever.

Even in judgment, God drew a picture of a coming day when His Son would come to pave the way back to the Father. And centuries later, Jesus arrived on earth proclaiming the time had come. He would defeat Death and reunite us with His Father and ours, making a way for all who believe in Him to get back to their true and eternal home in God's Presence.

Those were crazy, audacious words in the ears of mortals in Jesus's day, and they can be hard for us to grasp, too, but they tell of a divine plan formed from the foundation of the world and illustrated at the garden's gate.

In our Father's hands, what the devil perceived as his big win contained the hidden seed of his coming defeat. Let that speak to us right where we are: The enemy's plans against us are powerless to thwart God's promises for us. Consider the glistening words of James, penned after the death, burial, and resurrection of Jesus, his stepbrother and our Lord: *Mercy triumphs over judgment* (James 2:13 NASB).

Yes, and amen. Because Death lost at the cross, we don't have to live in fear of it. *O death, where is your victory? O death, where is your sting?" The sting of death is sin, and the power of sin is the law; but thanks be to God, who gives us the victory through our Lord Jesus Christ* (1 Corinthians 15:55-57 NASB).

I love knowing God's cosmic clock was ticking on our enemy's victory lap from the get-go! Instead of tossing man aside like Eve must've have pitched away that damning and darkening fruit, the love of God doubled down. Access to His presence was now guarded, but see the wonder of mercy—mankind wasn't discarded!

Now That's a Bouncer!

Even as God was sending the couple out of Paradise, He was illustrating how He would one day provide the way back to His presence. But about that illustration. We left the cherubim and flaming sword barring the entry, and I promised to show you the glory in the scene. Let's go back and see it together.

So, He drove the man out; and at the east of the garden of Eden He stationed the cherubim and the flaming sword which turned every direction to guard the way to the tree of life (Genesis 3:24 NASB).

Fascinating. I'd love to have the full scoop on these celestial beings, but the Word stops with one tantalizing description: two angels and a fiery sword. Oh, throw this storyteller a bone, Lord!

What did these supernatural bouncers look like? How big were they? Were they clothed? If so, what were they wearing? Did they have on shoes or were they barefoot? What were they saying? Or were they singing? Were they speaking at all? Perhaps they were silent. Yes, that seems appropriate. Silent and imposing. What about emotion? Did they have expressions? Did they look happy, sad, angry, hopeful, or what?

We could gather up all the descriptions of cherubim in the entire Bible and still not be able to nail down a clear picture of this angelic sentry. Oh, we could mine a few common denominators, enough facts to conclude cherubim are winged creatures with hands and feet. After that, the gaps are obvious and mysterious.

Our research would tell us some cherubim have one face, but some have two, and others have four! Some have two wings, others have four, and some have six! We would learn cherubim are often depicted in Scripture as hybrid creatures with characteristics of humans and animals. (Unless they're not.)

When shown with multiple faces, we'd see how some of the faces are human while others resemble lions, bears, and bulls. My over-active mind can supply visual on top of visual. You? And yet, mystery upon mysteries, God tells us cherubim are stationed at the gate. Full stop.

I can't tell you why we're given so few angelic details, but I have a theory. I think Scripture is intentionally vague in describing the cherubim wherever they're mentioned so we'll focus on what angelic visitors are *doing* instead of becoming engrossed with their appearance. God knows better than any of us how prone we are to worship what we see with our physical eyes! It wouldn't be uncharacteristic of us mortals to fixate on angels instead of on the One Who deploys them, or we wouldn't have the following passage from Colossians.

Let no one keep defrauding you of your prize by delighting in self-abasement and the worship of the angels, taking his stand on visions he has seen, inflated without cause by his fleshly mind (Colossians 2:18 NASB).

Ahem. With that warning, let's look at what Scripture does tell us about cherubim.

The word *cherubim* comes from the Akkadian term *karub*. It refers to the guardian of a divine throne. Wherever we find cherubim in Scripture, we see them guarding access to God's Holy Presence, just as they're doing here at the gate. They've been charged with barring access to the Tree of Life and keeping fallen man out of the garden where he enjoyed the intimate Presence of God. No doubt these supernatural sentries would be an intimidating sight all by themselves—but wait, they're not alone!

Stationed between this otherworldly security team stands a flaming sword turning in every direction. A sword ever moving, a sword on fire without flaming out. The fiery image begs us ask, "What is this?" But according to Scripture, "Who is this?" would be the better question. In the sixth chapter of Ephesians Paul identifies, the sword of the Spirit as the word of God.

And take the helmet of salvation, and the sword of the Spirit, which is the word of God (Ephesians 6:17 NASB).

Apostle John reiterates: Jesus is this living Word of God. Jesus is the sword of God's mouth.

In the beginning was the Word, and the Word was with God, and the Word was God (John 1:1 NASB).

And I saw heaven opened, and behold, a white horse, and He who sat on it is called Faithful and True, and in righteousness He judges and wages war. His eyes are a flame of fire, and on His head are many diadems; and He has a name written on Him which no one knows except Himself. He is clothed with a robe dipped in blood, and His name is called The Word of God. And the armies which are in heaven, clothed in fine linen, white and clean, were following Him on white horses. From His mouth comes a sharp sword so that with it He may strike down the nations, and He will rule them with a rod of iron; and He treads the wine press of the fierce wrath of God the Almighty ... (Revelation 19:11-15 NASB)

God pronounced the penalty for the couple's sin. Jesus, the Flaming Sword, stands ready to enforce it. What a scene. The writer of Hebrews also describes this sword.

For the word of God is living and active and sharper than any two-edged sword, and piercing as far as the division of soul and spirit, of both joints and marrow, and able to judge the thoughts and intentions of the heart. And there is no creature hidden from His sight, but all things are open and laid bare to the eyes of Him with whom we have to do (Hebrews 4:12-13 NASB).

Whoa. The Sword that divides and judges every heart and lays them all bare before God is positioned here to stand guard at Eden's gate! Guilty and exposed, Adam and Eve must have quaked before this fearful Flaming Sword. My knees would've been totally knocking. Right about now, I wouldn't blame you for thinking, *Uh, Shellie, can you get to the good part? You mentioned the promise of this scene?*

I understand. The picture is uncomfortable. That's because you and I come to God standing right there with Adam and Eve, on the wrong side of this most fearful of all "Keep Out" signs along with every person who has ever drawn breath. We're all on the outside looking in, and this much is clear: We'll need a miracle to pass through this flaming portal. Someone will have to come from the land of Paradise into the land of Death and bring us home.

Someone did.

Take heart, writer.

Take heart, reader.

Our Savior and this fearful sight standing guard at the gate of Paradise are the same. There's our promise in the scene! The Sword executing God's judgment is the Lamb who bore the weight of it at Calvary. Our Judge is our Justifier, the Guard is our Deliverer, and the Fiery Blaze lights our way home! Adam and Eve knew life deep and wide with God. You and I are born trying to get back to it. The glorious truth of the Gospel is that Jesus made a way. Jesus *is* the way.

Jesus said to him, "I am the way, and the truth, and the life; no one comes to the Father but through Me." (John 14:6 NASB)

God not only made a way for us to return to Paradise, He provided for something better. What could be better than living in a protected paradise, visited by God? How about becoming a dwelling place of God where He is always present? How about a lifetime membership that doesn't hinge on what we do but upon Whom we believe? That would be way better, right? The dreadful vision of the cherubim and flaming sword point to this very promise. They speak of Jesus, the Door to Heaven, the One who would create a way back into the friendship of God.

Centuries later when Jesus came to earth, He proclaimed, *"I am the door; if anyone enters through Me, he will be saved, and will go in and out and find pasture."* (John 10:9 NASB)

This flaming double-edged sword at the garden's entry is the Word of God, which both cuts and heals. The Fearsome Warrior in the book of Revelation riding the white horse, judging and making war against all unbelievers, and the Sword of God, Who circumcises the hearts of believers and reconciles them to His Father and ours, are one and the same. The Way, the Truth, and the Life stands here at Eden's gate. Behold the promise of the fearsome scene! Jesus, Immanuel, God with us. His body, the veil through which we pass to reach God.

Hebrews 10:19-20 tells us that believers approach God by the *blood of Jesus, by a new and living way which He inaugurated for us through the veil, that is, His flesh* (NASB).

We're looking at the triumphant foreshadowing of mercy. God had a plan to redeem fallen man from the outset, and it necessitated closing off the garden lest man live forever in his fallen state. And yet, even as He sealed it, God planned a way for us to return to Him.

Today, you and I are invited back to God through Jesus, the flaming passageway. Only this time, God planned for our hearts to be His garden sanctuary. He purposed to come and dwell with us here and now, through His Spirit, in the good and hard moments of our lives on earth, and afterward for all eternity. We are right now His garden. Our hearts, right now His happy place.

A garden shut up is my sister, my bride (Song of Solomon 4:12 ASV).

And the Lord will continually guide you, And satisfy your desire in scorched places, And give strength to your bones; And you will be like a watered garden, And like a spring of water whose waters do not fail (Isaiah 58:11 NASB).

The finished work of Christ says you and I can enjoy the privilege that Adam and Eve forsook. We can walk in this life with God. Where man was once walled out, through Christ Jesus we've been walled in with God, sealed for all eternity.

Do not grieve the Holy Spirit of God, by whom you were sealed for the day of redemption (Ephesians 4:30 NASB).

We were made in God's image, and Jesus came in ours, to live, die, and live again. He made a way for us not only to have the privilege of a relationship with our Maker that Adam enjoyed but for our experience to begin at our new birth and never, ever end. He created a garden in our hearts where we can die to ourselves and live in Him, beginning now. That's the holy dare embedded in finding the deep and wide life—dying to ourselves. We'll be breaking that down together soon. Right now, I have a question for each of us to consider.

Adam and Eve couldn't believe God was enough. What about us? Will we go about our waking-up, falling-asleep, running-around, working-hard-playing-harder lives discovering the ever-increasing delights of His Presence, or will we follow the first couple's ill-fated example?

We can spend our lives agreeing with what God says is good and choosing well, or we can spend our days forfeiting the best to grasp for all the rest—for the people, places, things, and circumstances we determine we must have to be satisfied, happy, and wise.

The two trees are always before us. Will we learn from Adam and Eve's mistake, or will we continue to repeat it?

Questions for Group Study or Private Reflection

1. In your own words, explain why God was merciful in sending the couple out of the garden.
2. How does it impact your thinking to consider your heart to be God's garden?
3. How do you feel after seeing the choice outlined between believing God is best and God is enough or continuing to search for fulfillment short of His company?

Chapter Seven

·····

Grandpa, Tell Me 'Bout the Good Old Days

"Refuse to be average. Let your heart soar as high as it will."

—A. W. TOZER

My daughter and daughter-in-law are gifted young women. Among their many talents, they're both excellent cooks and crafters. They enjoy finding an image on Pinterest and replicating it in their own style. As do I. This came as something of a surprise to the girls when I first brushed off my crafting skills to join them.

I felt compelled to tell the sweet young things of a time, long, long ago, back in the day when they were taking afternoon naps at preschool, when yours truly was quite the competent crafter. I explained how we earlier crafters didn't have it as easy as they do now. We didn't have access to huge crafting stores or endless websites at our fingertips filled with ideas.

"Oh, no," I informed them like a wise old owl. "We stomped through the woods and braved head-high snow drifts to scavenge for our materials!"

You're right. That wasn't entirely true. I was having fun with the girls as I described the good old days in glowing terms. It's what a lot of us do. Even (and maybe especially) we church people. Take our Woe is the State of the World parties. Maybe you've thrown a few of these gatherings, or perhaps attended a couple. But I'm doing my best to avoid them these days, and here's why. Indisputable evidence of our eroding culture surrounds us, but we shoot ourselves in the gospel feet if all we talk about is how dreadful things have become and how good they used to be! Helping to spread that brand of woe means our Gospel-purposed feet, meant to bear the good news, serve only to distribute more hopelessness!

Worse still, of those listening to our woeful words, the very ones needing to hear the good news are likely to get bored, defensive, or both, and tune us out before we can ever get to the blessed Gospel of Christ.

I've got another plan, and I can back it up with God's Word. Let's be real about the state of the world without burying the good news of the Gospel at the tomb of yesterday's golden memories by clinging to promises like this one: *The Law came in so that the transgression would increase; but where sin increased, grace abounded all the more . . .* (Romans 5:20 NASB)

Super-abounding grace in the face of very real sin was the glorious reality presented there in the garden at sin's initial strike. Promise given even as punishment was handed down.

Sin found a place in Eve, spread to Adam, and snared all of humanity, but Grace appeared in the middle of their mess—and He lives in the midst of our sin-reeling world, too. This is the news we're meant to share without sticking our heads in the sand and proclaiming all is lost for the rest of the world while "the few, the proud, the saved" live on doctored memories of days gone by.

As a storyteller, I can get lost thinking about the many tales Adam and Eve must have passed down in those earliest years after the Fall.

My imagination can run wild wondering what they said and what they didn't say about that sad day in Paradise when they were kicked out of the garden.

I wonder if they had to be peppered with questions before they would talk about *the incident*. Did they grow quiet whenever conversation turned to the dreadful choice that changed their lives forever? Maybe they skimmed the painful stuff to share the sweeter memories, what it was like for Adam to name the animals with God and how the Creator and the created chuckled over the pronouncement of "hippopotamus." "God liked that name. I remember Him saying, 'Good one, Adam.'"

And yet, light-hearted moments aside, I can also see Adam and Eve getting weepy when they talked about the garden. I know hindsight is said to be 20/20, but when I talk about the past, I tend to see it through a nostalgic filter. My family would vouch for my rose-colored glasses. But Adam and Eve didn't have to embellish their garden stories for the wow factor or whitewash the glory days before the Fall. It was enough for them to recount the facts of what it was like to walk with God when all truly was well, until it wasn't.

The horrors of the Fall and the grace that surrounded it would've been enough to mesmerize their listeners. If ever a story needed "just the facts" telling and retelling, it was this one. For as surely as the first family tree began to branch, each subsequent generation lived and died one step further removed from the very real garden and the God who walked and talked with them there.

Oh, the stories Adam and Eve could tell, and the progression! They could testify about Death entering their world that dark day when they first chose their will over God's. They could tell how Death began its hideous reign from the moment they chose to do their own thing over what God had deemed the best thing. I imagine their tales featured heavy doses of remorse over all they had forfeited, which begs a question: Of those who heard, was anyone listening? I can hear it now.

Yeah, yeah, Adam. I remember this part. It's when the snake started talking, right? I've never heard a snake talk and neither has anyone else I know.

True to human nature, Scripture suggests most of Adam and Eve's descendants turned deaf ears to their garden stories. And yet, it also provides us with a tantalizing biography of one notable exception who may have been paying attention, for he definitely embraced the possibility of walking with God on this side of heaven instead of waiting for eternity. We can find his story in the fifth chapter of Genesis, in the middle of a vivid illustration of the death march that began with the Fall. It's a somber listing of successive generations of people who lived, had babies, and died. Repeat. And then, smack-dab in the middle of this most morbid monotony, we're introduced to one who didn't die. Ever.

Meet Enoch.

Enoch lived sixty-five years and became the father of Methuselah. Then Enoch walked with God three hundred years after he became the father of Methuselah, and he had other sons and daughters. So all the days of Enoch were three hundred and sixty-five years. Enoch walked with God; and he was not, for God took him (Genesis 5:21-24 NASB).

That last line! My mind races with questions at those words: *And he was not, for God took him.*

Do tell.

How did God take him? From where? And most importantly—why?

Thanks to the detailed account of that death march from Genesis 5, even someone who has trouble balancing a checkbook (shout out to my husband, a.k.a. the beloved farmer, for deciphering my bookwork year after year) can deduce Adam, who lived past the age of nine hundred, was somewhere in his middle years when baby Enoch was born; Scripture clearly tells us Adam lived another three hundred years after Enoch's arrival. My point? Enoch the Enigmatic had plenty of time to hear his great-great-great-great-grandfather's stories! Consider the implications.

The same Adam with the glory stories of what it was like to live in the garden and enjoy open and easy friendship with God shared time and space on Planet Earth with Enoch of disappearing-act fame. Did Adam's testimony stoke Enoch's desire to seek and know God for himself? It seems probable, at the very least.

I once ran across a cool old tale that said God and Enoch were out walking and talking one day when they realized the day was ending and they were closer to God's house than Enoch's. The story says God and his good friend Enoch just decided to stroll on to Heaven. While mere conjecture, I find the story enjoyable because the biblical record of the friendship between Enoch and God teases us with its lack of details. But back to the scriptural account.

Two times in Enoch's short bio, the Word notes that Enoch "walked with God." And while our story of Enoch and God ambling home is sweet, the Bible uses the phrase "to walk" to indicate so much more than a stroll. It depicts a way of life. To walk with someone suggests camaraderie. *Do two walk together unless they have agreed to do so?* (Amos 3:3 NIV)

To walk can mean to pursue or to follow, but it always carries themes of unity, communication, and forward progress. Walking takes us further with every step. This is the life of faith Jesus promises. Not a dreary wait-and-see existence where we come to faith and then hunker down until we're taken out of here., but the start of an every-day journey, human hand in divine hand. This is how Enoch lived before he disappeared without a trace.

If the Genesis account is fascinating, the next mention of Enoch comes from the New Testament book of Hebrews and totally stirs the mystery.

By faith Enoch was taken up so that he would not see death; and he was not found because God took him up; for he obtained the witness that before his being taken up he was pleasing to God (Hebrews 11:5 NASB).

It may be my storytelling nature, but to say Enoch wasn't found implies someone searching for him.

"Hey, Billy Bob, have you seen Enoch?" (I'm pretty sure Billy Bob wasn't a common name back in the day, but it's fun. Work with me.)

"No, not lately, why?"

"Well, no one has seen Enoch since last Friday when he said he was going for a walk to talk to God. You don't reckon? I mean, you don't suppose … ?"

"What?"

"Oh, nothing … I'm probably being silly …"

As intriguing as Enoch's brief bio is, I've brought you his mysterious, short-on-details story to celebrate one undeniable truth that can rock our little spiritual worlds if we'll let it. I'd never be able to build up enough drama for the following announcement, so I'll just say it: This incredible slice of human history, of a man walking so closely with God that His Maker took him to Heaven without ever seeing death, happened *after* the Fall, *after* man was expelled from the easy, intimate, automatic, ongoing presence of God, *after* access to the garden was roped off by those mighty cherubim and that Flaming Sword, and *before* Christ came.

Do tell.

Enoch lived after the Fall and before Christ. Before God came in the flesh, before man beheld His glory in the face of Christ. Sit with that a moment.

If anyone's life depicts the "deep and wide" relationship with God we're talking about here, it's Enoch's.

I don't know about your Christian experience, but that level of intimacy with God blows the doors off what I've been conditioned to anticipate in my faith journey. I've been assured I can and should pursue God here in the twenty-first century, but the idea that He and I could enjoy the sort of deep relationship He evidently had with Enoch? Come on! We're not told we can't, but we aren't encouraged to believe we can, either. That's for a chosen few like Mother Theresa and Billy Graham, right? Wrong.

That's a devastating lie. It makes us incredulous about a reality the Bible teaches us to expect, and it encourages us to settle far below our birthright. It's why I love the gospel of John. It's impossible to read John without wondering about the discrepancy between the experience of the average believer and the one Jesus promised, the one I'm daring us to pursue!

[H]e who loves Me will be loved by My Father, and I will love him and will disclose Myself to him (John 14:21 NASB).

That's not me making up a pie-in-the-sky promise. That's Jesus promising to reveal Himself to those who love Him.

We can ignore those words and make excuses for why we're not experiencing them. Or we can quit letting the faith of those around us set the bar for our walk with God and refuse to settle for anything less than what He promised in His Word. We could pay less attention to what man says about God and more attention to what God says about men.

I've got one word for what will happen if we choose door number three: life-changer. (Okay, that's two words, but I hyphenated them.) My point? I believe you and I experience God in our daily lives to the degree that we desire and expect to experience God. Our relationship with Him will be as strong or as weak as our determination to know Him beyond the understanding we have when we first believe.

Too many of us cede our personal responsibility to seek God to the leadership of our preachers and teachers—and in relinquishing our personal pursuit of God, we relinquish the promise of Christ: namely, life in His Presence where He regularly discloses Himself to us personally.

Enoch's story is concrete evidence of God's enduring desire to reveal Himself to His creation and have them walk in His company—after the Fall. All is far from lost if we can dare to embrace Enoch's story and allow ourselves to consider what all God has provided for us in Christ Jesus and refuse to settle below it. We can ask ourselves what we're missing because we've allowed men to set limits (intentionally or not) on how intimately we can know Him on this side of Heaven, and we can resist their religious perimeters.

We can, and I have. As we say around these parts, "Stick a fork in me, I'm done." That's South-mouth for "I'm through having my God expectations mandated by man." I'm hungry to experience everything I can of who He is. And God's Word couldn't be any clearer on this topic. Those who long for an intimate knowledge of who He is aren't after anything His great big heart hasn't already made available.

The Mystery of More

Over and over in the Scriptures, God expresses His intention to be our God and for us to be His people. The variation of this phrasing I love the most is His often-expressed desire to "be God to you." It's mentioned first in Genesis 17:7. God is talking to Abraham when he says, *"I will establish My covenant between Me and you and your descendants after you throughout their generations for an everlasting covenant, to be God to you and to your descendants after you."* (NASB)

I'd underline and star those five incredible words: *to be God to you*. Whatever that fantastic promise includes, it's one of God's go-to expressions. He uses those words or similar phrasing more than three hundred times in His Word.

Having God be God to us is a tantalizing offer. We'll never come to the end of that mystery on this side of Heaven, but we can begin to unwrap it by allowing Enoch's epic disappearing act to challenge us. His life speaks to a deeper level of friendship with God than I have at this writing, but it's a relationship Scripture puts forth as available to each of us. Let's ask the Holy Spirit to help us respond to God's intense love for our company with a passion for His! God has more for all of us, whether we're new followers or mature believers.

How can I be so audacious as to include you when I don't know if your faith is deep and wide or narrow and shallow? Because, wherever we are in our faith, God has yet to walk us out of this world and into the next one without tasting death! *And since God hasn't transported our physical bodies to Heaven to be with Him there, I'm crazy enough to believe we can draw nearer to Him here!*

Wouldn't you just love to know how Enoch grabbed God's mighty heart like that? I'm grateful Scripture doesn't leave us guessing on this one! The Spirit of God penned the answer for us in the book where we're told Enoch "wasn't found" in Hebrews 11:6.

By faith Enoch was taken up so that he would not see death; AND HE WAS NOT FOUND BECAUSE GOD TOOK HIM UP; for he obtained the witness that before his being taken up he was pleasing to God. And without faith it is impossible to please Him, for he who comes to God must believe that He is and that He is a rewarder of those who seek Him (Hebrews 11:5-6).

First, I didn't go all caps on that line in verse five. That was the NASB translation, and I love using it here because I think the announcement deserves some emphasis, too!

It says Enoch had the reputation of pleasing God, but some of your translations might say Enoch was "known to walk with God." That's more than okay. The Greek translation of "pleasing to God" is the very same Hebrew phrase that means "walk with God"!

That's bigger than it sounds, but I sense some eye rolls. (It's a gift. I trace it to motherhood where eyes-in-the-back-of-the-head insight develops out of necessity.) Perhaps you're thinking, *But, Shellie, we already know Enoch walked with God from our Genesis story. What are you driving at?* Hang with me. We're about to connect some serious dots.

Why was Enoch's faith walk pleasing to God? The answer is in verse 6, where it says it's impossible to please God if we don't believe He rewards those who set out after Him. If Enoch pleased God, we can conclude, without stretching the Scripture, that he lived his life not only pursuing God, but believing God was taking note of his quest!

That's epic good news for us, because the mindset that set Enoch apart from those around him can set our lives apart, too! Enoch lived to know God, he believed God was aware of his pursuit, and he expected God to reward his faith. Let that be jet fuel for your faith.

You and I won't be content to warm a pew if we're convinced God wants to warm our hearts!

By the way, among the scant details of Enoch's life Scripture records another golden nugget. The famous disappearing man had sons and daughters! Really? So, Enoch didn't live his life like a monk, secluded on a mountaintop before God, sitting cross-legged and humming? Not if he had a family life and all the responsibilities that come with it. Interesting. That means Enoch must not have mailed in his missionary musings from his favorite retreat center. You know, the one with the gorgeous view and endless pot of coffee. (We're getting real, now.)

Give Me Jesus Time and No One Gets Hurt

I'm sort of known around these parts for saying, "Give me Jesus time and no one gets hurt." I'm just joking, of course. Kinda.

Backstory? Several years ago, I was scheduled to speak at a large conference in West Monroe, Louisiana. The weeks leading up to the big day found me spending time with the Lord and preparing notes for my turn at the mic when He up and played a joke on me.

Please don't let that offend you. I'm not being irreverent. I promise. He may not mess with y'all, but He messes with me on a regular basis. (Granted, I ask for it! But that's another story, and I'm trying to stay on point.)

The short of it? I got this whole download of something I can only liken to a Christian rap (with apologies to rap artists everywhere.) The words just came and kept coming. A younger girlfriend told me I'd written something called a word story. Okay. The point is I wasn't asking for it. I was born with a beat in my feet, but I can't carry a tune with both hands. I was sure the good Lord had meant to send the message to Toby Mac or Lecrae, but no—I got it. Keggie, grandmother of five. Don't even try to tell me God doesn't have a sense of humor.

I had zero intention of reciting my new free verse at that large conference, and I wouldn't have, only the Lord wouldn't quit weighing on me with His mighty thumb. In the end, I gave in, and there at the close of my remarks, before God and everybody, I debuted that word story, called *Give Me Jesus Time and No One Gets Hurt*. You can still find footage of that moment floating around the internet, but I'll spare you and wrap it up here. (Wrap—not rap.)

The free verse was me admitting I don't live at a retreat center, either. I need Jesus in the worst way, every day. I can bring home the bacon and fry it up in a pan. I can be our family's cook and social director, secretary and cab driver. I can be mother, daughter, wife, sister, grandmother, friend, all of it—if my eyes are on Jesus. I must have Jesus. Saying "give me Jesus and no one gets hurt" isn't me condoning violence. It's my humorous way of encouraging all of us to own and celebrate our shared and sacred need. We must have the One who birthed our faith to sustain it.

A getaway with God can be just what He prescribes in a given season, but we're not called to retreat from our daily lives to know Jesus! We're called to retreat with Jesus, to be much alone with Him and then to walk about holding Him in our hearts, listening for Him and yielding to Him as we go. We're given the privilege of finding Him here with us in Monday's messes and Thursday's troubles—if we're intentional about looking.

Enoch the family man couldn't have withdrawn from everyday life to walk with God. Clearly, he welcomed God into his daily comings and goings even as he walked among the flesh-and-blood people that surrounded him. This was Enoch's habit, and it changed his life. It holds the power to transform our lives and the lives of those we love, too.

Storytime, anyone?

As I was writing on this passage, I got crossways with someone in my immediate circle of family and friends. I'm talking about a level of frustration that tempts a person to hash and rehash a conversation long after it's over. My own words challenged me to believe God was willing to get in this business, too.

Did it take longer to surrender to that truth than I would've liked to admit? Afraid so. Sadly, I can still be stubborn and rebellious enough to live in the ugliness of circular thinking when I know full well He'll pull me out of the muck if I'll unclench my fists and reach for Him.

I hope that confession won't move you to close the book on me (pun intended), but I haven't yet made it to a place where I'm always saintly, and I don't live with unlimited patience for those around me. The sole difference is that I now understand how quickly darkness can creep in and consume my thoughts if I refuse to expose them to the Light. I've discovered the immeasurable benefit of owning up to how much I need Jesus and asking Him for help over, again, and constantly.

I can't recommend this life of running to Jesus strongly enough. When we openly acknowledge our inability to live *for* Him without drawing *from* Him, we get to pull from the bottomless well of resources that are ours in and through Christ Jesus. Does that sound like a good theory? Well, let's go back to this morning's frustration and see what it looks like in practice.

I could've stayed in that frustrating, guilt-inducing, familiar cycle of asking the Lord to forgive me for what I was thinking about the other person and then having to ask Him again the next time my thoughts slipped off the high road and went back to devising a stellar comeback for our next confrontation. (I know every rock, pebble, and mud hole on that road!) Instead, I surrendered my *right* to my offense and called on Jesus to help me break the cycle of my thoughts. I asked Him for grace to forgive that person because He forgives me. And whenever I found myself stuck in the muck, again, I ran right back to that deep, deep well, again. He met me there, every time, without once scolding me for my neediness. He did, however, give much-appreciated perspective. He's faithful like that. When we ask Him to teach us how to do life, He does. So don't push pause. Don't have someone "hold your earrings" and don't "grit your teeth and bear it." Reach for the Inexhaustible Jesus.

Our neediness isn't news in Heaven. Jesus merely pours out His grace anew because, unlike our good intentions, His mercies never run dry. Victory isn't us trying. It's Immanuel doing. Oh, the pressure-busting Presence of God that guards a mind given over to Him! I wish I could pack this peace up and hand it to you, but I can't wrap the Almighty, and the peace I'm describing doesn't exist outside of Him.

Be anxious for nothing, but in everything by prayer and supplication with thanksgiving let your requests be made known to God. And the peace of God, which surpasses all comprehension, will guard your hearts and your minds in Christ Jesus (Philippians 4:6-7 NASB).

The Lord is near. I could give you plenty more examples from my own life, but here's another from a friend. One morning Shawna (not her real name) found herself having a silent rant in her head with her husband as Target Number One. It was one of those chaotic mornings where she was trying to get the kids to school and herself to work, and, as she saw it, her man wasn't doing enough to help. Soon, she was ruminating over a whole list of his faults, past and present, none of which had anything to do with the morning's routine and the incident that first annoyed her. Things were deteriorating quickly when Shawna began thinking about what she was thinking about, and that caused her to hit the brakes and turn her thoughts to Jesus.

She asked for holy help to restrain her mouth and yield her thinking. Like me, she may have asked several times, and as with my experience, Holy Help came each time. In a text she dashed off to me later, a surprised Shawna reported that not only did her 911 praying eventually diffuse her mental monologue, but she soon found herself appreciating some things her husband *does* do to help which, until that moment, had not even been on her radar!

That's more than just a good story. It's solid biblical principle.

Choosing to turn our eyes to Jesus always opens our ears to more Truth while resisting Him sears the conscience and leaves us vulnerable to more whispers from the enemy.

Therefore consider carefully how you listen. Whoever has will be given more; whoever does not have, even what he thinks he has will be taken from him (Luke 8:18 BSB).

Think about the volume on a laptop or phone. When we choose our own words or actions over what we know God has said or is saying, we may as well "mute" His voice. Delayed obedience is rebellion still, and it brings the danger of no longer hearing what God is saying because we're resisting what He already said. Do you want to mature in Christ more quickly? Obey more quickly. Obedience is a hearing aid.

It was no accident when Shawna began to mentally rehearse other marital aggravations. The enemy was happy to supply additional ammo. Satan stalks us to discover our sore spots, and then he works relentlessly to get us to hide them in our hearts and pamper them ad nauseum. He wants to keep us nursing the wound and running from sweet Jesus instead of sprinting into His outstretched arms.

Sometimes we'll ask for strength to not act on our impulses ahead of a situation, and sometimes we'll ask for forgiveness when we blow it. Both responses are good, but what we desperately need to learn is how to holler "Help!" in the middle of the mess!

For we do not have a high priest who cannot sympathize with our weaknesses, but One who has been tempted in all things as we are, yet without sin (Hebrews 4:15 NASB).

Jesus understands our weakness and inadequacies. He wants to come alongside us through His Spirit who lives in us and show us the way out of turmoil and temptations! We're often blind to the exit. We don't even know how or what to say to Him in prayer, but His Spirit does, if we'll call to Him for the help we need.

That's what Shawna did. She stopped the downward spiral when she threw the brakes on the thought train, opened her ears to God's Voice, and found fresh perspective to de-escalate the drama. It's the power of choice. We have fresh opportunities to choose well all day, every day.

These are just a couple examples of how God wants to be in it all with us, the big things and the small. And (oh, someone is going to have to help me celebrate this next truth) this offer of divine friendship is all inclusive!

Consider that Enoch's friends and family could've walked in God's intimate company the same as Enoch did! You and I may be prone to favoritism, but we have biblical assurance that God isn't!

Opening his mouth, Peter said: "I most certainly understand now that God is not one to show partiality, but in every nation the man who fears Him and does what is right is welcome to Him." (Acts 10:34-35 NASB)

God has embraced the world through Christ Jesus. The potential to respond to Him lies within reach of us all.

Before he left this world, Enoch tried to wake up those around him. According to the book of Jude, Enoch tried to warn them that God was paying attention and would one day require an account of their lives, but his preaching fell on hardened hearts.

By way of reminder, we're searching the Word for flesh-and-blood people who lived the holy dare, those who found the deep and wide. Generations would come and go before anyone would walk so closely with God that the Great Record-Keeper would pen another such biography.

Questions for Group Study or Private Reflection

1. Can you think of a way you may have been conditioned, even by well-meaning believers, to expect far less from your walk with God than what Adam and Eve experienced in the Garden of Eden?
2. Do you think you've ever relinquished your personal pursuit of God to settle for what other flesh-and-blood people tell you about Him? If so, explain.
3. What does it mean to you for "God to be God to you"?

Chapter Eight

· · · · ·

Living the Dream No Man Had Seen

S ay hello to Noah. You've heard his story. He's a familiar character with a tall task, and he comes on stage at one of mankind's lowest lows. We might not be able to hear the dirge playing in the background when Noah arrives on the scene, but it's a dark period on Planet Earth.

Then the LORD *saw that the wickedness of man was great on the earth, and that every intent of the thoughts of his heart was only evil continually.*

The LORD *was sorry that He had made man on the earth, and He was grieved in His heart. The* LORD *said, "I will blot out man whom I have created from the face of the land, from man to animals to creeping things and to birds of the sky; for I am sorry that I have made them."* (Genesis 6:5-7 NASB)

Evil was rampant, and God was through. He was ready to do away with everyone.

Almost. There was that one man living in a way that caught God's divine eye.

But Noah found favor in the eyes of the LORD. *These are the records of the generations of Noah. Noah was a righteous man, blameless in his time; Noah walked with God* (Genesis 6:8-9 NASB).

I remember the details of a picture I first saw in a little Sunday School room at Melbourne Baptist Church in Alsatia, Louisiana, when I was no more than five or six. The print was mounted in a simple frame on our classroom wall. It depicted a scene from the Great Flood. Heavy rains were falling, water was rising, the ark was floating, and people were pounding in vain at the huge wooden door. From my vantage point in an itty-bitty chair at a mini-table, the whole thing was horrifying. The only emotion the picture inspired in me was fear of this God my teacher said had shut that mammoth door that no man could open. Not even Noah, had he been inclined to do so.

I took that fearsome depiction of judgment deep into my soul. For years afterward, fear of divine wrath combined with my desire to escape it was my sole motivation for serving God. I wanted to appease God enough to escape judgment, but I wanted to live for myself, (see Chapter One). All I got for those religious efforts was a sense of always trying and always falling short.

What I was super-slow to understand is true for all of us: Trying to serve God from what we consider to be a healthy distance will always leave us malnourished and empty. Attempting to serve God without drawing from Jesus is soul-draining religion. Run from it.

God wants to be our satisfaction. He wants us to experience Him in the middle of it all so He can be all to us and in us—and ultimately, so He can extend life through us. For in experiencing the life-giving source that is Christ in us, we become a life-giving source to others. Noah's life is a great illustration of this truth.

If we'll keep reading beyond Noah's introduction and his ark-building call from God, we'll see a striking observation about this man. In addition to the record of Noah walking with God, Scripture notes Noah is the *only* man God saw as righteous in his entire generation.

Then the LORD *said to Noah, "Enter the ark, you and all your household, for you alone I have seen to be righteous before Me in this time."* (Genesis 7:1 NASB)

Have you ever felt like you're the sole one trying to do the right thing? I think we're all susceptible to "poor pitiful me" parties. The problem is we're reliably lenient on ourselves and critical of others, and our judgments are questionable. This is Truth Himself vouching for Noah, and God declares him to be the sole righteous man alive. That "attaboy" isn't meant to condemn us. On the contrary, it can be faith-building good news. Noah's relationship with God saved his life and his family's lives and preserved humanity on earth. He was the invisible God's very visible testimony. We're meant to be that, too.

Remember how we pondered the influence Adam's garden memories must've had on Enoch? Consider the impact Enoch and the legend of his great disappearing act would have had on his great-grandson Noah! I'm thinking that whole "He was here and then he wasn't" story was one Noah might have heard more than a few times over the years. How would he have been impacted by hearing that his great-grandfather walked so closely with God that God walked his friend out of this life without seeing death? Impacted enough to build a huge boat on dry ground, in a land that had never seen rain fall from the sky? Maybe.

We don't know how Enoch's life shaped Noah's ark-building, generation-saving faith, but the very idea can move us to ponder our lives and ask ourselves how we're impacting the course of our own family lines. Could our descendants be inspired to live monumental, earth-shattering, remarkable lives because you and I walked with God? Absolutely. Our stories are being written in glory before the eyes of our Creator, right along with Adam's, Enoch's, and Noah's.

Malachi 3:16 reads, *"Then those who feared the LORD spoke to one another, and the LORD gave attention and heard it, and a book of remembrance was written before Him for those who fear the LORD and who esteem His name."* (NASB)

You and I can be those in this present generation who walk with God and grab His great big heart by learning how to lose our religious mindsets and live coming and going with Jesus. Bonus? Our lives will offer a tantalizing appetizer of God to everyone around us.

Before we go any further, however, let's restate the major premise of these early chapters: *We can trust that however much we want to know God, His desire for our company exceeds our desire for His.*

Yes, the Fall sliced through the paradise man shared with God and their sweet fellowship was broken, but remember how quickly God pointed to the day it would be restored. And yes, man turned further and further away from God until the Flood fell and erased all but one God-fearing man and his family. But the waters of justice couldn't douse the fiery passion in the Creator's heart for His created any more than their disobedience could prevail over His immeasurable love in the garden. Stay tuned. We'll soon see mercy triumph over judgment yet again.

I'm eager to keep tracking God's great desire to settle into our nine-to-fives instead of coming and going in what we deem to be our sacred moments. Because He doesn't come and go. He abides with us. He promises to never leave us. Our challenge is learning how to live in Him, with Him, and before Him.

As the pages of Scriptures turn, we'll see how our determined God in all His fierce, unceasing, relentless love has never once stopped coming for His people. He comes for us still.

Questions for Group Study or Private Reflection

1. Think of a time when listening to truth opened your ears to more truth, or vice versa. What was that like?
2. Do you come from a family of believers? What impact has their faith had on yours? If you don't have that history, write a couple sentences about the type of legacy you'd like to leave for those coming after you.
3. Using your Bible's concordance or the search engine of your choice, find a verse of Scripture that speaks of God's relentless love for His people and determine to memorize it so you will have it close.

Chapter Nine

Bring Your Broken Want-To

*"Grace is the voice that calls us to change and then
gives us the power to pull it off."*

—MAX LUCADO

My mama is the genealogy buff of our family. She's traced our tree like a detective, and she speaks the language of greats and great-greats and second and third cousins twice removed with ease. I don't have that gift, as evidenced by her ongoing amazement. "That's your great aunt's cousin's younger brother's sister's child, Shellie! I can't believe you don't remember her!"

Shortcomings aside, I'm stretching my genealogy credentials to set up the next biblical record we have of anyone responding to God's passionate desire to walk in intimate friendship with us because it comes with the introduction of Noah's great-great-great-great-great-great-great-great-grandchild, Abram. (That was eight "greats" if you weren't counting. I spelled them out to help us grasp how many people lived and died since God rebooted the earth with a flood and Noah and his people stepped off the ark.) And yet we have no record of anyone pursuing God in the whole-hearted ways of Enoch and Noah until the arrival of Abram. We're introduced to Abram in a just-the-facts passage at the end of Genesis 11.

Now these are the records of the generations of Terah. Terah became the father of Abram, Nahor and Haran; and Haran became the father of Lot. Haran died in the presence of his father Terah in the land of his birth, in Ur of the Chaldeans.

Abram and Nahor took wives for themselves. The name of Abram's wife was Sarai; and the name of Nahor's wife was Milcah, the daughter of Haran, the father of Milcah and Iscah.

Sarai was barren; she had no child. Terah took Abram his son, and Lot the son of Haran, his grandson, and Sarai his daughter-in-law, his son Abram's wife; and they went out together from Ur of the Chaldeans in order to enter the land of Canaan; and they went as far as Haran, and settled there. The days of Terah were two hundred and five years; and Terah died in Haran (Genesis 11:27-32 NASB).

If our minds strayed reading that passage, we may have missed Abram. The man destined to become the father of the Christian faith gets the briefest of introductory bios. It's more about Abram's daddy than Abram. Joshua 24:2 records these words*: Thus says the Lord, the God of Israel, From ancient times your fathers lived beyond the River, namely, Terah, the father of Abraham and the father of Nahor, and they served other gods* (NASB).

Abram's father worshipped idols with the rest of his hometown. That's interesting. It's not found in the biblical account, but Jewish tradition says Abram's father was also an idol merchant. That means he worshipped the very gods he bought and sold. What? Terah served the same gods he was trading? Who does that? Well, for starters, I can. And you can, too.

I don't want to lose the thread of the story we're weaving, but I need to say this: If the words I write that turn into the books I sell come to mean more to me than my relationship with God, my work is an idol, and I'm trading it on the open market at the expense of my soul. (Gulp!) I commit to hearing and heeding that warning. Whatever we're living for is what we're worshipping. What dreams, goals, or goods are you buying and selling that have the potential of becoming idols in your life? Here's a dire warning from the book of Jonah on this ever-present pit:

Those who cling to worthless idols forfeit the grace that could be theirs (Jonah 2:8 NET).

Forfeited grace. Remember when we talked about getting more than you bargained for? Let's reread that verse substituting whatever we're tempted to run after for the word "idols." Whatever fills our blank causes us to forsake what we're truly longing for—the grace, mercy, and steadfast love of God.

According to Jewish tradition, Abram was just a child when he first began questioning the legitimacy of the idols his family and culture considered gods. One story is told of young Abram taking a hammer while his father was away from the shop and smashing all the idols except for the largest one. Afterward, he propped the hammer in the remaining idol's hand. When his father returned and discovered his merchandise had been destroyed, he turned to his son for an explanation. Without hesitation Abram told his father the largest idol had smashed the smaller statues. Indignant, the older man informed his son they both knew an idol could do no such thing.

Legend has it young Abram replied, "Then why do we worship them?"

Why, indeed? I can't imagine anyone worshipping the things around them while they neglect the Creator behind it all, can you? Oh. Right. But about Abram ...

Those same Jewish sources record Abram coming to believe in one Creator God who was over everything instead of the plethora of gods his people worshipped. Neither biblical account nor historical record tell us how Abram came to believe in this one true God. What we do know, and we'd do well to remember, is regardless of *how* Abraham came to believe, the gift of faith *to* believe came from God Himself. We're each given this gift to embrace or reject.

For through the grace given to me I say to everyone among you not to think more highly of himself than he ought to think; but to think so as to have sound judgment, as God has allotted to each a measure of faith (Romans 12:3 NASB).

To recap, we have a summary of where Abram fits in the family tree, and we're told he's living in the land of Haran with his father, his nephew, and his barren wife. Oh, and there's that one cryptic insertion about Sarai not having children, which is an interesting by-the-way suggesting the couple's ongoing disappointment, but beyond that, nothing remarkable is said of Abram. No character description, no buildup, nothing to prepare us for the call of God in the next chapter. Chapter 11 simply ends with Abram's father dying in Haran before Chapter 12 opens with Abram's famous invitation from God:

Now the LORD *said to Abram, "Go forth from your country, and from your relatives and from your father's house, to the land which I will show you; and I will make you a great nation, and I will bless you, and make your name great; and so you shall be a blessing; and I will bless those who bless you, and the one who curses you I will curse. And in you all the families of the earth will be blessed."* (Genesis 12:1-3 NASB)

Without any fanfare, we see God telling Abram to leave everything familiar to him and strike out into the great unknown where God promises He'll bless all the families of the earth through his lineage, although Abram has no children. Wowza. No destination? Not even so much as a physical address to type into his smartphone? I can't be the only one who wonders how exactly Abram heard that divine instruction. Was it an inside voice, an outside voice, a gut feeling? The record is brief, otherworldly—and supremely characteristic of God.

You're looking at one of God's great signatures. He neither explains Himself nor debates His existence with any of us. Why? Perhaps the first chapter of Romans holds the best answer.

[B]ecause that which is known about God is evident within them; for God made it evident to them. For since the creation of the world His invisible attributes, His eternal power and divine nature, have been clearly seen, being understood through what has been made, so that they are without excuse (Romans 1:19-20 NASB).

We often complain of not understanding what God is asking of us. God insists everything we need to know to follow Him has been revealed to us and in us. It boils down to this:

He is God. We are not.

God states that He exists and that He has given evidence of Himself in the world around us and in our individual hearts. Our choice is as old as the Garden of Eden. We can acknowledge Him and walk with Him in what promises to be a need-to-know type of relationship, or we can reject His claim as our sole authority and pursue our own goals and dreams.

When you put it that way, Abram's heavenly invitation isn't so different from Adam and Eve's—or yours and mine. Our response determines whether God will make our hearts His home. Abram's life-transforming choice was to believe God and go.

As they walked together, God continued to elaborate on His initial promise to Abram. When they reached Canaan, God changed Abram's name to *Abraham*, meaning "father of a multitude of nations" and Sarai's name to *Sarah*, "mother of nations." Then he made Abraham another promise: He would give his descendants the land where he was standing.

Descendants? God continues to talk about descendants to Abraham and Sarah, who are now senior citizens and still childless. Can you even imagine their late-night pillow talk? You can read about their challenges to believe God would put a baby in an old woman's womb in Genesis 17, but the Bible records that through it all, Abraham chose to believe and say *yes* to God's Word.

Abraham didn't get the full picture from Day One. But finally, we see the famous promise God made to Abraham that would change everything for all of us:

"Indeed I will greatly bless you, and I will greatly multiply your seed as the stars of the heavens and as the sand which is on the seashore; and your seed shall possess the gate of their enemies. In your seed shall all the nations of the world be blessed, because you obeyed my voice." (Genesis 22:17-18 NASB)

God first promised Abram land, then He promised him descendants, and finally, He promised to bless those descendants. That's revelation on a need-to-know basis, step by obedient step. It's another example of the truth we saw in the last chapter and yet another reminder of how He will speak to us. God reveals more to those who respond to what He has already said. We will get revelation in our lives the same way Abraham did: by obeying what has already been revealed. When we dare to trust and act, we get more light. Where will that light take us? How closely can we follow? The Bible says no man has seen all God has planned for those whose hearts are fully His.

But just as it is written, "Things which eye has not seen and ear has not heard and which have not entered the heart of man, all that God has prepared for those who love him" (1 Corinthians 2:9 NASB).

I once thought (or perhaps I was taught) that this verse spoke of the life after this one, but since I've come to understand Jesus *is* eternal life, I've changed my mind. I believe it speaks of the open-ended discovery of looking and listening for Him now.

But about the big promise God made to Abram. Let's be candid. It doesn't necessarily get our blood going, does it? If you've ever secretly wondered how an ancient promise made to a man long dead matters in your twenty-first-century life, I get it. And it's vitally important we address it because, regardless of the subject matter, if you and I don't understand what's in it for us and why, we'll lose interest sooner rather than later. You know I'm right.

So, if you get that, hear this: God's promise to Abraham holds even greater potential for our lives than it did for the faithful patriarch and his kin. That's not my claim. It's God's Word. The New Testament spells out our inheritance in Abraham's centuries-old promise through our present-day faith in Jesus Christ.

And if you belong to Christ, then you are Abraham's descendants, heirs according to promise (Galatians 3:29 NASB).

We've inherited Abraham's blessing. That's great news, but we find the "more better" part in Hebrews as the writer celebrates the more excellent ministry of Jesus, the better covenant He mediates on our behalf, with its better promises.

But now He has obtained a more excellent ministry, by as much as He is also the mediator of a better covenant, which has been enacted on better promises (Hebrews 8:6 NASB).

We get a better covenant with better promises? Yes! With our personal stake settled, let's take another look at just what God promised us and how deep and wide it can actually get.

"I will establish My covenant between Me and you and your descendants after you throughout their generations for an everlasting covenant, to be God to you and to your descendants after you." (Genesis 17:7 NASB).

God pledges Himself to Abraham and to his descendants (that's us!) and promises Abraham He will "be God to him and to his people." There's the delightful phrasing we mentioned in an earlier chapter. I'm sure I understand only a fraction of those words, but I love the sound of them. At the minimum, having God "be God to me" suggests He will employ His every power, provision, and attribute on my behalf, consider my every request, and respond according to what is best for me from His all-knowing perspective.

By all accounts, Abraham liked the sound of God being God to him, too. When God told Abraham to leave his family and go, Abraham went. When God said He would make him the father of a nation, Abraham believed Him. When God said Abraham would bear a son in his old age when his wife was past childbearing years, Abram considered everything that could mean for two aging seniors well past their baby-making prime and chose to believe again. In return, God called this man His friend.

Was not Abraham our father justified by works when he offered up Isaac his son on the altar? You see that faith was working with his works, and as a result of the works, faith was perfected, and the Scripture was fulfilled which says, "And Abraham believed God, and it was reckoned to him as righteousness," and he was called the friend of God (James 2:21-23 NASB).

What a saint, this man. If only we could believe like Abraham, right? But wait, y'all. We can! It does us forgiven-but-flawed believers no good to pick and choose mountain-moving highlights of Abraham's much-vaunted faith without considering the full account of his story. The Bible doesn't record Abraham as a man who believed God without ever having to deal with his doubts. I can't speak for you, but I need to know that.

Abraham isn't the father of our faith because he never doubted. He is the father of our faith because He didn't allow his doubts to prevail. Despite what he could see, Abraham learned to trust the One he couldn't see. I'm reminded of some of my favorite words from Peter: *Though you have not seen him, you love him. Though you do not now see him, you believe in him and rejoice with joy that is inexpressible and filled with glory ...* (1 Peter 1:8 ESV)

Let's steep our souls in the fortifying truth of Abraham's full story. This man wasn't born with mighty unshakable faith. The Word says he grew in it!

In hope against hope he believed, so that he might become a father of many nations according to that which had been spoken, "SO SHALL YOUR DESCENDANTS BE." Without becoming weak in faith he contemplated his own body, now as good as dead since he was about a hundred years old, and the deadness of Sarah's womb; yet, with respect to the promise of God, he did not waver in unbelief but grew strong in faith, giving glory to God, and being fully assured that what God had promised, He was able also to perform. Therefore IT WAS ALSO CREDITED TO HIM AS RIGHTEOUSNESS.

Now not for his sake only was it written that it was credited to him, but for our sake also, to whom it will be credited as those who believe in Him, who raised Jesus our Lord from the dead (Romans 4:18-24 NASB).

Abraham considered his elderly body and that of his wife, stacked the facts against the promise of God, and chose to believe. And then he chose to believe again and again as he grew in his faith. We have before us the same choice when confronted with circumstances that don't agree with what God has promised in His Word. We can consider the situation, give glory to God, and grow stronger in our faith, or we can waver in unbelief. God doesn't ask us to deny our circumstances. He asks us to trust Him despite them.

By the way, every single word of promise God made to Abraham came to pass in record-breaking time!

Wait, what?

Not really. I was just seeing if you were paying attention. That's how you and I like things to happen, but Abraham's story takes a ton more twists and turns. Just like ours. If our twenty-first-century lives were added to the Word, the answer to our heartfelt prayer from yesterday might come in the next chapter, or it could show up twenty chapters later.

Will we continue to believe when the only evidence that God has heard is His promise that He's listening? That's what Abraham banked on, according to the passage we just read in Hebrews, and the couple did welcome that promised son into their home—wait for it—in their twilight years! Burp rags and brown spots? I feel you, Sarah. I'd love to chase that rabbit, but we're about to hit the gas again on our trip through the biblical timeline.

For the record, I realize we're racing through Bible history at breakneck speed—but the closer we get to seeing how God has extended to us the wholly restored and yet unparalleled offer of walking in intimate friendship with Him on this side of Heaven, through the person of Jesus Christ, the harder it is for me to slow down. At the same time, I remain convinced there's great benefit in seeing the consistency of God's desire for our company as witnessed down through the ages by people just like us.

We won't find anything in the Scripture that even faintly suggests God has abandoned His desire to walk in the very midst of His created beings like He once did in the garden of Eden, but we can find plenty reason to believe He is as eager to be God to us as He was to Adam and Eve. From His earliest interaction with man, God has shown Himself to be a personal Being who enjoys revealing Himself to those who look for Him.

My ongoing experience? A mediocre search produces average discovery, but an unrelenting pursuit brings unparalleled rewards.

You will seek Me and find Me when you search for Me with all your heart (Jeremiah 29:13 NASB).

Back to our narrative. After four hundred years of slavery in Egypt, God reached down and handpicked a man from Abraham's descendants by the name of Moses to fulfill both His own great desire to live among His people and His covenant promise to Abraham.

God would personally make a way to lead His people out of bondage and bring them unto Himself.

Questions for Group Study or Private Reflection

1. Shellie says whatever we're tempted to run after can be an idol in our lives. What's yours? (It's okay to use coded language only you would understand if you're worried about someone finding your notes.)
2. What did it mean to you to learn that Abraham faced doubt, same as us, but chose to believe? Did it change your perception of the father of our faith? If so, how?
3. On a scale of 0 to 10, 0 representing total disinterest in God and 10 an unrelenting quest, where would you put yourself?

Chapter Ten

· · · · ·

When God Plays Pictionary

*"Joy . . . is an unceasing fountain bubbling up in the heart;
a secret spring the world can't see and doesn't know anything about."*

—DWIGHT L. MOODY

The way my husband, Phil, plays Pictionary will frustrate you to no end—if you're on his team. However, if you and your bestie are on the same side and Phil is paired with her husband because you and she are smart like that, you will get to laugh all night long. If you believe life can be hard when it's good but it's always better when you're laughing, you'll want to play Pictionary with Phil and Lamar, often. Bless 'em. (Just try not to be on their team.)

Phil is notorious for giving you one drawing—one. Regardless of what he sketches, you'll need to guess what it's supposed to be from that single image. To be fair, Phil will help you as the clock ticks down by circling the picture repeatedly. He'll also tap his drawing with his pen and grimace at you, as if you're the one holding the team back.

We're about to see God play Pictionary with the children of Israel, but unlike my beloved famer, God excels at illustration. (Sorry, Phil! You can't be good at everything!)

This is where we could take a detailed look at when and how Moses led a huge mass of people like you and me out of Egypt. (The estimate is somewhere around six million!) Only this is not that book. We could study about a stubborn Egyptian pharaoh reluctant to release his slaves. We could read about the pestilence, plagues, frogs, and flies Almighty God used to change the emperor's mind. We won't. Not that those things aren't packed with powerful lessons. They are, but I'm trusting you know the bare-bone stories of how God put His mighty hand into the land of Egypt and extricated Abraham's descendants. (You can find the complete story in the book of Exodus.)

Since we're in the middle of tracing God's forever desire to be God to us and we're trying to figure out how to live responding to His great big heart, we're going to skip ahead and join the Israelites en route to the Promised Land. Slavery lies behind them, and the promise of the good life looms somewhere ahead of them (so says Moses.) They've followed God out of Egypt, but their old lives in Egypt are still following them. Nod if you resemble that.

Who is this God who rescued them? What makes Him tick, and whatever does He want from them? Sound familiar? It should. Watching God interact with these newly delivered pagans who had been living in a foreign culture with nothing more than hand-me-down stories of His dealings with their ancestors until they were chosen as undeserving recipients of His love can be a powerful help to us. For that's precisely where we are when God brings us to Himself.

But now in Christ Jesus you who were formerly far off have been brought near by the blood of Christ (Ephesians 2:13 NASB).

Having been born of His Spirit, we're no longer far off from Him. He lives with us and we belong to Him as surely as Abraham's recently rescued descendants belonged to God, but we come into this relationship as a group of similarly confused refugees, clueless about how to walk with Him on this side of His chain breaking remake of our lives. Who is this God who breathed new life into us, anyway?

We can learn a lot about our new life in Christ by watching God teach this dysfunctional family of His how to live with Him. There'll be remedial lessons because God's people have something of a hearing and retention problem.

Much like someone trying to communicate with another person who doesn't speak his language, we'll watch God bend down and begin to draw pictures for His people. It's the original Bible Pictionary, and here's the best part: If we listen, we'll be able to hear Him wooing us as He instructs them. We'll see the glorious Gospel of Jesus Christ lit up and lined out. We'll see what He has already done for us and the fullness of all He wants to do in us.

It'll be easy enough to identify with the Israelites. They'd just left a foreign culture that, despite being full of hardships, was all they knew. And they were being called out of everything familiar by a God whose ways were as foreign to them as His image was invisible. They'd bought into the idea of the Promised Land Moses was selling but soon found themselves walking in circles trying to find it and grumbling with every step. Hello, church. Welcome to Growing Pains 101.

The children of Israel saw God guide them by day with a cloud that offered shade (think "umbrella at the beach") and they experienced Him warming their bones every night with a fire that offered warmth and light (think "night light for an anxious toddler"). Still they whined, worried, and doubted. They'd seen God meet their every need, yet they seemed determined to make a career out of complaining and whining. (Mirror, mirror, in our hand.)

For the record, I didn't come up with the childhood analogy for God's people. "The children of Israel" is a biblical term, and Scripture isn't referring to a group of chronological babies marching out of Egypt. It's picturing a much-loved infant nation God took to Himself. God uses this language in the book of Hosea, too. In what must be one of the most tender passages in all His word, God grieves over His wayward kids.

When Israel was a child, I loved him, and out of Egypt I called my son. But the more they were called, the more they went away from me. They sacrificed to the Baals and they burned incense to images. It was I who taught Ephraim to walk, taking them by the arms; but they did not realize it was I who healed them (Hosea 11:1-3 NIV).

I get Israel's pouty problem. Perhaps you've never had a child-sized, stomp-your-baby-foot moment with God because you've prayed 'til your pray-er is falling out, it doesn't look like He is coming through for you, and you're worried He won't. Maybe you've never had a time when the memory of what He has done for you in the past is hard to hold onto in the face of what you need Him to do for you now. I have. Thankfully, our doubts don't alter God's faithfulness.

If we are faithless, He remains faithful, for He cannot deny Himself (2 Timothy 2:13 NASB).

But about our cohorts. We're jumping back into the story, a few months after their exodus from Egypt. They've set up camp under the leadership of Moses at the base of a mountain named Mount Horeb, and their ever-faithful, ever-attentive God has settled in at the mountain's peak and invited their point man up to His place for a get-together.

Interesting side note? This mountain was the scene of Moses's burning-bush experience where God had first called him to lead His people out of Egypt (Exodus 3:1-12). Moses and six million of his closest friends have now arrived at the very spot where God had instructed Moses to go get His people. Talk about a full-circle moment.

Something momentous is about to happen at this mountain, again. Until now, God has not required much of the fledging nation. He's fed them and guided them—exactly like we do for our helpless infants. And like spoiled children everywhere, they'd grown increasingly demanding by the time God sent Moses an intimate invitation to meet Him at the top of the mountain. It was time for a heart-to-heart, or what we in the South call a "come-to-Jesus meeting."

We can find that divine meet-and-greet in Exodus 19:3-6.

Moses went up to God, and the Lord called to him from the mountain, saying, "Thus you shall say to the house of Jacob and tell the sons of Israel: 'You yourselves have seen what I did to the Egyptians, and how I bore you on eagles' wings, and brought you to Myself. Now, then, if you will obey My voice and keep My covenant, then you shall be My own possession among all the peoples, for all the earth is Mine." (NASB)

If you'll allow me some freedom, the incredible message God gives Moses to take down to the people could be loosely translated, "If you'll be mine, I'll be yours."

Message in hand, Moses descends the mountain to bring God's invitation to the people, who listen and respond with their own pledge of faithfulness. Scripture tells us Moses then returned to God to report: The people had heard and accepted His offer.

Will You Go Steady with Me?

That scene reminds me of grade-school courtships. The kind where your best friend brings you a sweaty love note from your secret admirer. Back in the day, we called it "going steady." I know, it's an outdated term, but boy did your heart melt when the right person asked you to go steady!

We tend to read these passages as if the people hearing God's words were emotionless robots, but they were people who longed to be loved and protected. Just like you and me, they wanted to be wanted. The love-note visual might be grade-school, but the truth pictured in Moses's back-and-forth between God and the people illustrates the eternal good news of Jesus Christ.

Jesus is the mediator between God and man Who was sent to earth with a divine offer on a Heaven-sent mission. *Namely, that God was in Christ reconciling the world to Himself, not counting their trespasses against them ...* (2 Corinthians 5:19 NASB). That's Jesus, literally dying to take our hands and put them back in His Father's. Think on that while we slide back into our scene.

Commitments exchanged, God proceeded to give Moses something like "The Big Ten House Rules for Relationship," along with a more detailed breakdown of His expectations. You might recognize the house rules by their more formal name: The Ten Commandments.

I don't relish telling the next part of the story, but it's necessary. Even as Moses was meeting with God, the people at the base of the mountain were demonstrating their waning interest in Him. The whole thing was taking far too long, and they were going back to what they knew. Ouch. Think of it as SADD (Spiritual Attention Deficit Disorder). You won't find that in the medical journals, but it affects all of us at one point or another. But back to the distracted desert dwellers.

Their idol worship would be the well-known incident that birthed the golden calf and led to Moses having a massive hissy fit that was recorded for all time. In righteous indignation at the people's flagrant disobedience, Moses took the stone tablets with their holy commandments engraved by the very finger of God and threw them to the ground, breaking them into pieces (Exodus 31:18).

It's another ugly moment for man and another heart-stopping opportunity to behold the inexhaustible love of God! Even with God's first written law lying in shards at man's feet, God's intentions to be God to His people couldn't be thwarted.

Amazing Grace, He loved them still.

Amazing Grace, He loves us still.

Once Moses confronted the people and cleaned house, so to speak, God called him right back up to the mountain and gave him a fresh set of commandments. And He also gives him something else.

Drum roll, please.

To tutor His people, God opens Relationship 101 by drawing pictures for His relationship-challenged offspring. He instructs them on the building of a portable temple, where they'll come to worship

Him. And through that temple's detailed design, He begins to illustrate the foundation for their new life, demonstrating how they could meet with Him, in a physical location, through an appointed man.

I'm trying to think like my editor and pace myself here, but it's hard. (Editors are big on thought progression, and my books are the better for it!) Besides, I'm determined to give you biblical evidence of the glorious reality of God's forever plan to dwell in our getting-up-and-going-to-work lives, rather than simply telling you it's possible to do daily life with Him, but every word of our historical jaunt keeps pointing to Jesus. Take the last line of the paragraph above—in a physical location (put a hand over your heart) through an appointed man (thank you, Jesus!). See what I mean?

As surely as God showed His ancient people how to build a place for Him to dwell with them, God provided a better place for us—where you and I can not only meet with Him, but live with Him in our physical bodies through one appointed man, the God Man, Jesus Christ. God's Presence in the Old Testament temple and all its instructions point to this privilege, and it's ours on this side of the cross. Tuck that in your heart. I've got another encouraging heads-up before we delve into God's sketches.

The Israelites are given all kinds of instructions, from how to choose the right turtledove for temple sacrifice to how long one should stay out of the sanctuary after childbirth. But you and I won't need a single turtledove to get in on the day in/day out glory of an intimate life lived with God. On the contrary, every carefully drawn picture of the Temple and the Heaven-instructed worship offered on its holy altar pulses with the good news of the Gospel.

Jesus fulfilled every single requirement of the law on our behalf! Jesus not only met and exceeded the bar for all of us, for all of time, He obliterated it. He put us in God's favor and made it possible for us to walk with Him and His Father on this green earth, just like Adam and Eve, Enoch, Noah, Billy Graham, and any other supersaint that comes to your mind! Oh, believer, don't despair if you feel weak in faith. Rejoice to kneel at the Cross's even ground with the greatest saints who ever drew breath! Their inheritance is yours! Don't bemoan your little faith, just refuse to stay there!

Here's another reason to exhale. We won't be embarking on an in-depth study of the temple and its furnishings. (I need to sit in on such a study, not teach it!) We'll be training our focus instead on the temple's most sacred item: the Ark of His Presence.

Remember when we talked about Noah's answering God's call to build an ark and the refuge it offered him and his family during the storm? Here in the wilderness, God instructed His people to build another ark. It would be known by several names, including the Ark of His Presence, the Ark of Testimony, and the Ark of the Covenant.

We're going to see how the promise of God's Presence accompanying the Ark is our promise of living with God, unboxed, so to speak, in the middle of our everyday lives. And we'll unpack the how-to of such living that's forced on no one but open to all. From the onset of the temple-building process God put spectacular emphasis on the people's free-will participation.

This Ark will represent *the very place* where God would come and dwell among His people, and just like Noah's big old boat, it's built from a heavenly blueprint, too. God gave Moses instructions on how to build this sacred meeting place and travel with it. Let me rephrase that in a more faith-fortifying way: We'll watch God teach them how to go about their daily lives, carrying His Presence.

Instructions on how to carry about His Presence. That makes my pulse quicken. You? Everything about this ark illustrates God's passionate determination to live in our midst. It may be an ancient set of blueprints but, if we let it, the story of the Ark can shake us out of our religious comfort zones and help us take the holy dare of refusing to settle below God's deep, wide promises. Life spent in pursuit of God is anything but boring. Adventurous? Sure. Dry? Not on your life!

Questions for Group Study or Private Reflection

. . . .

1. Describe a scenario that makes you doubt God even though He may have shown Himself faithful in that very area before.
2. Give an example from your own life of how you are more familiar with the ways of the world than you are with God's ways.
3. Take a few minutes today for an online search on the Ark of the Covenant to prepare for the next chapter. Note one thing you learn from your study.

Chapter Eleven

. . . . .

Lights, Action, Truth-Telling?

"Behold the Lamb of God who takes away the sin of the world!"
—JOHN THE BAPTIST

It was 1981 when *Raiders of the Lost Ark* hit the big screen, in which a bookish archaeologist named Professor Indiana Jones embarks on a mission to recover an ancient artifact of the Israelites known as the Ark of the Covenant. My super-big hair and I (rumor has it we took up two seats) were swept up in the fast-paced adventure with scores of moviegoers as the mild-mannered professor morphed into a swashbuckling, wisecracking hero right before our eyes. Indy wanted that storied ark, and he was willing to face down bad guys and lay his life on the line to secure it!

In the movie, the Presence of God accompanying the ark is depicted in a special-effects, hold-onto-your-sticky-theater-seats type of moment. The excitement around the ark builds throughout the film until, at last, we're presented with it. Indy finally gets his hands on the sacred artifact—just in time to have the bad guys appear and snatch it away! Bummer, right? No worries. Let's keep watching. The bad guys are about to make an ill-advised move that will end their criminal careers.

Whether from ignorance of the Ark's history or pure disrespect for its sacred nature, the bad guys pry the lid off the holy chest and are exposed to the supernatural power it contains. As a rush of glory from within the Ark literally melts the faces off the bad guys, the good guys (our beloved Indy and his sassy love interest) save themselves by shielding their eyes from the divine danger.

Breathe out, moviegoers, all is well.

The make-believe world of Indiana Jones did a commendable job in depicting the story of that ancient chest and the power of God's Presence accompanying it. Our purpose has been served. Pull the lights up, and let the credits roll.

While *Raiders of the Lost Ark* was all Hollywood with lights, action, and make-believe drama, the legend of the original Ark is biblically and historically sound. The Old Testament Ark of the Presence was both God's chosen resting place among the ancient Israelites— and a gloriously illustrated message of a greater reality available to us today! It holds an all-important answer to the "what now" questions we have once we come to faith.

The Ark was built per God's own instructions and carried one forevermore exciting and extremely personal pledge to His people. Let's train our eyes on those instructions. We'll find the blueprint in Exodus 25: God instructs Moses on how the people are to build Him a temple, designed according to the pattern He showed him on the mountain, a physical sanctuary where God Himself intends to dwell. *Let them construct a sanctuary for Me,* **that I may dwell among them** (Exodus 25:8, NASB, emphasis mine).

In verse 25, He further pinpoints where He plans to rest. *"You shall put the mercy seat on top of the ark, and in the ark you shall put the testimony which I will give to you.* **There I will meet with you** from above the mercy seat ..." (Exodus 25:21-22 NASB, emphasis mine).

"That I may dwell among them."

"There I will meet with you."

God is making Himself clear. He's not content with guiding His people from afar and being worshipped from a distance. He means to take a seat in their midst, in the very thick of things.

When God Takes a Seat

As newlyweds, my man and I embarked on life with a limited number of furnishings. These weren't aged antiques handed down from our ancestors but run-of-the-mill hand-me-downs. Neither of our family trees included the sorts of aristocrats that might bequeath stately bed frames and hope chests. Not that Phil and I were complaining. We had each other, and we had the necessities. Table, bed, refrigerator, and, of course, that one irreplaceable piece high on every man's must-have list, a recliner. Once we positioned it in its special place, our house became a home.

We were kids about to have kids. We had zero idea of all the living that would center around that beefed-up rocker. At first, it was just my beloved farmer and I snuggling there. Over time, we began to rock our babies there. And every day, once his work was finished, the man of the house would take a seat in the center of the family he loved.

When God began to give Moses instructions for the furnishings of the special house where He would dwell among His people, He started by commissioning a seat for Himself, too. It was literally called God's Mercy Seat, and it was a designated place where He promised to recline.

Just as Phil and I couldn't imagine how much living would revolve around that old recliner of ours, I'm convinced the Ark illustrates a depth and breadth of relationship God desires to have with us that's mindboggling in its intimacy and beyond our dreams. Let's read the portion of Scripture describing the biblical ark.

Let them construct a sanctuary for Me, that I may dwell among them. According to all that I am going to show you, as the pattern of the tabernacle and the pattern of all its furniture, just so you shall construct it. They shall construct an ark of acacia wood two and a half cubits long, and one and a half cubits wide, and one and a half cubits high. You shall overlap it with pure gold, inside and out you shall overlay it, and you shall make a gold molding around it (Exodus 25:8-12 NASB).

We've just read about the very first item God commissions for the temple: a small wooden rectangular box overlaid with gold. Why didn't He start by telling the people how to construct the outer courtyard where they would enter the temple grounds, or maybe the brazen altar where they would make sacrifices for their sins? My answer isn't definitive, but we won't go wrong celebrating this observation: God initiates relationship with man. God loves first, and always.

We love, because He first loved us (1 John 4:19 NASB).

Again, God's number-one priority for furnishing the new temple was the Ark of the Covenant, and it was no make-believe movie prop. It'd be a man-made ark all right, but it was a replica of the original, existing outside of time, in an otherworldly place. Hebrews 8:2 tells us the sanctuary and everything commissioned for it were patterned after heavenly originals God had shown Moses during their meeting on Mount Horeb.

Then the Temple of God in heaven was opened, and the ark of his covenant was seen inside his Temple. There were flashes of lightning, noises, peals of thunder, an earthquake, and heavy hail (Revelation 11:19 ISV).

God pulled back the invisible curtains between this world and the next to allow Moses to see into His throne room and get the blueprint for the Ark. And that mercy seat we read about that God instructed Moses to place on the top of it? It's nothing less than a picture of Jesus. Romans identifies Jesus as God's living, breathing Mercy Seat.

... for all have sinned and fall short of the glory of God. But they are justified freely by his grace through the redemption that is in Christ Jesus. God publicly displayed him at his death as **the mercy seat** *accessible through faith* (Romans 3:23-25 NET).

Where verse 25 reads "mercy seat," your translation may use "propitiation" or "place of atonement." They're all the same, a seat of mercy where God accepts us through our faith in Jesus. Let's get an overview of what went on at this golden mercy seat so we can see how it pointed to what Jesus would one day finish on Calvary's hill.

To get a basic understanding of the sacrificial system God instituted for Israel to allow Him to dwell among them, we'll need to pan out to get a snapshot of the Old Testament tabernacle and temple grounds.

The temple grounds were formed by a rectangular structure whose walls were comprised of fabric coverings hanging from wooden pillars. Within this enclosed area, called the outer courtyard, stood a second, smaller rectangular tent, partitioned into two rooms. The first room a person entered was the outer tabernacle, or the Holy Place. The second, separated by a heavy curtain, was the inner tabernacle, or the Holy of Holies.

The priests regularly entered the outer tabernacle to make sin offerings for the people, but once a year, the High Priest of Israel went beyond that curtain into the Holy of Holies where the Ark rested. Known as the Day of Atonement, we find this annual event described in Leviticus 16. On this day, the High Priest applied the blood of a slain animal to the mercy seat to make atonement for the people's sins and allow Holy God to continue living among His unholy people for another year. With that bloody sacrifice, the people's sins were forgiven, removed, erased.

The imagery of this earthly mercy seat spoke of a day when Jesus, our great high priest, would cover the sins of all believers with His blood, once for all time, because He ever lives to make atonement for us. Over and again in the New Testament, Jesus revealed Himself as the fulfillment of God's promise to live in our midst. Jesus, our forever meeting place.

"If anyone loves Me, he will keep My word; and My Father will love him, and We will come to him and make Our abode with him." (John 14:23 NASB)

So this wilderness ark shows us Jesus? Let's see what else we can discover about it!

God continued with His building instructions:

"You shall cast four gold rings for it and fasten them on its four feet, and two rings shall be on one side of it and two rings on the other side of it. You shall make poles of acacia wood and overlay them with gold. You shall put the poles into the rings on the sides of the ark, to carry the ark with them. The poles shall remain in the rings of the ark; they shall not be removed from it." (Exodus 25:12-15 NASB)

Our golden box is designed to be portable! Underscore that. We'll come back to its significance.

"You shall make two cherubim of gold, make them of hammered work at the two ends of the mercy seat. Make one cherub at one end and one cherub at the other end; you shall make the cherubim of one piece with the mercy seat at its two ends. The cherubim shall have their wings spread upward, covering the mercy seat with their wings and facing one another; the faces of the cherubim are to be turned toward the mercy seat. You shall put the mercy seat on top of the ark, and in the ark you shall put the testimony which I will give to you." (Exodus 25:18-21 NASB)

In these verses, we see God commissioning Moses to form two golden angels and fit them on the lid of the mercy seat with their faces turned toward its center and their wings outstretched above it. And then, in verse 22, we find the promise we've already mentioned, along with a new one we haven't.

*"**There I will meet with you**; and from above the mercy seat, from between the two cherubim which are upon the ark of the testimony, **I will speak to you** ..."* (Exodus 25:22 NASB)

The emphasis is mine. I'd make it glow in neon lights if I could, for those promises transformed that gilded wooden box into the news of a glorious reconciliation. The garden has been long sealed, but God's desire to be with His creation hasn't waned. See Him here, providing a way for fallen man to experience life in His Presence again.

Today, the Holy One that met with Abraham's descendants above that physical mercy seat lives in the dusty frames of all believers. He desires to meet with us and speak to us, too, and it's all possible because of the costly sacrifice of Jesus, Lamb of God.

Remember our light-bulb analogy from Chapter One? We saw that we were made in the image of God and fashioned in a way that makes us capable of receiving His Spirit and becoming His dwelling place. This is what happens to us through faith in Jesus. Our circuits are reconnected, so to speak, and we inherit the promise of enjoying life in His Presence through Jesus our meeting place.

Jesus replied, "Anyone who loves me will obey my teaching. My Father will love him. We will come to him and make our home with him." (John 14:23 NIV)

Father and Son making themselves at home in us. Do we believe it? Better yet, are we experiencing it? Do we really expect Father and Son to eat breakfast with us tomorrow morning, run to the post office with us at lunch, sit with us while we turn in that big project, and accompany us to our loved one's funeral? Or do we persist in acting like God makes Himself comfortable in us only during our most holy moments, as we discussed earlier? Those moments after we've sung several worship songs, asked forgiveness for anything and everything we can think to confess, completed our daily Bible readings, and strung together enough prayers to be heard?

I can't say this enough because we can't hear it enough: God isn't merely putting up with us between our devotional moments. That's religion's evil lie, and it keeps us longing for God but living at a distance. We can't hear the truth enough because our enemy persistently peddles versions of that lie to keep us out of the transforming presence of God. It's why we must be equally committed to telling ourselves the Truth!

The staggering present-day promise of the Ark says all of life can be lived with God, through Jesus. If we can fully embrace this, Hollywood's special effects will seem flat-out puny and underplayed in comparison!

The otherworldly supernatural offer to meet with God through Jesus, the true Mercy Seat, is God's new and improved invitation to live in us and with us on this side of the Cross. We've been cordially invited to live in His company and enjoy Him forever, effective immediately. Not in the sweet by and by, not in our best moments, but right here in this everyday ordinary one where we may have been less than saintly a time or ten since sunup. It's not our performance or our intentions granting us this wide open and ongoing access. It's Jesus.

I could star that sentence with an abundance of exclamation points. I have good reason to be excited: Dying to all my trying has opened a whole new life for me.

I spent too many years of my Christian life feeling like God was with me when I was doing something I consider holy, but the rest of the time He was shouting distance away. Even after I decided I wanted Him in every part of my life, I couldn't figure out how to marry my "sacred life" with my "secular life," so I applied myself to Christian disciplines like daily Bible reading and prayer to please Him, then tried to act right when I was on my own time so He would "stay" pleased. It sounds so woefully ridiculous in print (not to mention embarrassing), but I'm determined to give you my honest experience, however silly or sad.

God and I didn't live together back then. We visited.

And if He felt distant when I tried to worship at church or during my prayer times at home, I would try to woo Him to return with the right words, posture, or attitude. As if I could woo the One who loves first, best, and always! Heads up: When we find ourselves acting like that, we're identifying more as a spruced-up guest house than God's chosen dwelling place, and that attitude will keep us from the well-blended life spent in God's presence we long to experience.

The Apostle Paul once penned a rhetorical question to the new believers of the Corinthian church. His words suggest the Corinthians were as slow as we can be in comprehending the full magnitude of life available to us through the finished work of Christ.

Do you not know that you are a temple of God and that the Spirit of God dwells in you? (1 Corinthians 3:16 NASB)

Today, I'm deeply grateful I've come to at least recognize the folly of trying to woo God, even if I do need the occasional reminder. I'm no longer content with head knowledge that God is always with me. I aim to live my everyday moments with my heart wide open to Him! I've been losing my religion for a good number of years now, and I like it. I want to live the privilege of walking and talking with God that Adam and Eve forfeited.

God is eager to keep company with you, too! If you could use some encouragement on that, stay tuned for a super-sized booster shot! The ark has much more to teach us. In the next chapter, we'll watch it come to life in blazing color in the work of Jesus, the gorgeous God Man. We'll begin to understand how Jesus makes it possible for us to enjoy life in God's Presence without getting our faces burned off (so to speak) by His very real glory.

What's more, we'll discover how to live with God without selling everything we own, saying goodbye to our people, and moving to a mountaintop. Holy seclusion never was and never will be a condition of His divine invitation. To live with God doesn't require us to ignore people. On the contrary! We're meant to bring His Presence into theirs.

I remember one day when God brought this home to me for the thousandth time. Three of our five grandchildren had spent the night. The next morning, as I walked into the kitchen to start breakfast, with the sounds of their voices coming from the great room, my thoughts turned to Jesus. I was hungry for Him. I remember wishing I could spend some time in prayer that morning but recognizing I was in an all-hands-on-deck situation with the littles.

That's when I heard Him. Oh, not in an audible voice, but in that deeper, louder inside voice I've come to recognize and love.

Bring them with you …

His voice was so gentle I resisted scolding myself for having to learn this truth yet again. Instead, I worshipped Him while we ate pancakes and I started a load of clothes. And because I was aware of His Presence with us, my grands were enveloped in His sanctuary with me. My guess is you need to hear this, too: God is with you. Quit waiting for quiet time. Life is wonderful, hard, satisfying, painful, sweet, and heart-breaking, and God wants to join us in the thick of it all.

Before we put *Raiders of the Lost Ark* back in the film vault, let's listen to some of the lines from the movie.

As the historical significance of the ark is being reviewed early on, the following snatches of dialogue hint at the adventure before Indy. As we read them, let's allow God to speak about the exciting quest ahead of us if we dare to accept His invitation to lose our lives to find them on this side of Heaven. These are just some of the legends and warnings mentioned in the movie pertaining to the Ark of the Covenant:

"Searching for the lost ark is not to be taken lightly."

"No one really knows all the ark's secrets."

"The ark is like nothing you've ever gone after before."

"The ark is not of this earth."

And finally, this: "The ark is a transmitter, a radio for speaking to God."

Wow. Truth, y'all, straight from a Hollywood script. I suppose stranger things have happened.

The biblical ark promised fallen man access to holy God. It was an ordained place to experience the One they knew from a distance, but it was a shadow of the far greater privilege to come, a day when man could host God's Presence, when he could become God's house instead of visiting it.

Our oldest grandchild is ten. Emerson is a natural conversationalist with a sweet nature and gentle ways. A good chat is right up her ally. Most all children start asking "why" as soon as they learn to talk, but Emerson's questions were on steroids. When she was just a toddler, I realized Emerson didn't care so much what we were talking about, as long as we were talking. I made up a game quite by accident that met her need to communicate. She caught on quickly, and the two of us could talk for hours about—nothing. I'll give you an example.

We'd be driving down the road and Emerson would pipe up from her car seat. "Keggie, why is that truck red?" And I'd say, "Because frogs are green." Emerson would giggle. "But, Keggie, why are frogs green?" And I'd say, "Because birds fly!" More laughter. "But, why do birds fly?"

You get the point. Discovering that Emerson's never-ending questions came out of her desire for conversation completely changed the way I looked at them!

Something similar happens when we begin to understand that "pray without ceasing" is not only possible, it can become delightful. Oh, sure, our analogy breaks down. Prayer isn't a childish game. But behind the Word's instruction to live in conversation with God is our loving Father, longing for us uncover the treasure of His daily friendship. He knows it holds pleasure beyond our wildest dreams.

Questions for Group Study or Private Reflection

1. What does it do for your faith to consider that God desires relationship with you more than you desire relationship with Him? Explain.
2. Look up several definitions of "mercy seat" and pen your favorite descriptive phrasing here. What draws you to these words?
3. Describe your current prayer life in one word.

Chapter Twelve

. . . . .

Like It Never Even Happened

The old covenant says, "Keep the law and live."
The new covenant is, "You shall live, and I will lead you
to keep my law, for I will write it on your heart."

—CHARLES SPURGEON

I'm taken right now with the tagline of a company that specializes in helping customers clean up after a disaster, such as a fire or flood: "Like it never even happened."

The commercials follow a pattern. A disaster has struck, and people are seen frozen in place as a team of experts descend with one goal in mind—total, brand-new-level restoration. The home or business is being cleaned up and repaired, its purpose reclaimed in record time.

While our immediate family hasn't needed those disaster cleanup services, and I say that with heartfelt compassion for those who have, the company's promise can set us up for a celebration ringing with eternal truth: All who come to faith in Christ Jesus are made brand-new, cleansed and restored. Though our sins be many, we're forgiven for all eternity. *Like it never even happened.*

It sounds too good to be true, but it's straight out of God's word. *For as high as the heavens are above the earth, so great is His loving-kindness toward those who fear Him. As far as the east is from the west, so far has He removed our transgressions from us* (Psalms 103:11-12 NASB).

Our sin, long gone, like it never even happened. We say we believe it, but do we live like it?

In my experience, it's easier to believe we've been forgiven of yesterday's sins than to embrace the promise of a life where we're being continually cleansed. And I think I know why. Being all too aware of how often we fall short of holy, it's hard for us to believe we can dwell with God all day every day, and in His favor no less. But we must remind ourselves of this truth because if we aren't convinced that we're *being cleansed,* just as we have *been cleansed,* the enemy will continue to cheat us of the joy of walking in friendship with Jesus on this side of Heaven. Truth says we live in God's favor through our faith in Christ's finished work, and we can't hear that often enough.

But if we walk in the light as He Himself is in the light, we have fellowship with one another and the blood of Jesus His Son cleanses us from all sin (1 John 1:7 NASB).

Note the present tense. We live being cleansed because the One who cleanses us ever lives. Jesus is the covering Who allows us to stand before God, the all-consuming fire, even as His Holy Spirit shapes our common human boxes into His dwelling place. And not just on Sunday when we're in church with our "best little believer" thing going, but on Thursday morning when God feels distant, we're confessing yet another failure, and we're secretly thinking God is justified for putting us in time out.

Christ constructs our lives as we voluntarily bring Him our daily decisions and choices. The Old Testament illustrates this through the temple-building instructions God gives Moses. Let's return to Exodus and take special note of the all-important specification God makes about those building materials and the way they're to be collected.

Then the LORD spoke to Moses, saying, "Tell the sons of Israel to raise a contribution for Me; from every man whose heart moves him you shall raise My contribution.

"This is the contribution which you are to raise from them: gold, silver and bronze, blue, purple and scarlet material, fine linen, goat hair, rams' skins dyed red, porpoise skins, acacia wood, oil for lighting, spices for the anointing oil and for the fragrant incense, onyx stones and setting stones for the ephod and for the breastpiece. Let them construct a sanctuary for Me, that I may dwell among them." (Exodus 25:1-8 NASB)

In specifying materials to be used for the temple, God says He wants them to be *voluntary contributions, given by those whose hearts are moved to give them.* I hope to explain the significance of that instruction by asking you a question or ten.

Do you know believers who never seem to grow beyond their initial come-to-faith experience, who never seem to mature spiritually even as they grow older chronologically? Perhaps you'd be so honest as to put yourself in that group. Take heart. Even if the description fits, you wouldn't be reading these words if you didn't want more, and you wouldn't want more if God wasn't drawing you deeper. So, no condemnation, just encouragement! But speaking of more …

Do you also know, or have you heard, of other believers who seem to put down roots in Christ Jesus and appear for all the world to be ever learning, constantly transforming, and growing more passionate about Him with time? Have you ever wondered what the difference is between those two Christian experiences? We're looking at a major clue.

Let's refresh our memories by looking back to that earlier scene when God rewrote The Big Ten and sent His commandments back down to the people, via his servant Moses.

Moses went up to God, and the Lord called to him from the mountain, saying, "Thus you shall say to the house of Jacob and tell the sons of Israel: 'You yourselves have seen what I did to the Egyptians, and how I bore you on eagles' wings, and brought you to Myself. Now, then, if you will obey

My voice and keep My Covenant, then you shall be My own possession among all the peoples, for all the earth is Mine." (Exodus 19:3-5 NASB)

Israel had said yes to becoming God's special people by agreeing to obey His voice and keep His Covenant. Think "mandatory ground rules." Now, as they set out to build God a dwelling place in their midst, the rules for engagement change dramatically. God commissions them to bring costly materials *as their hearts move them.* Oh, see the volunteer nature of this invitation! It's the difference between that always-growing, always-changing believer and the stagnant one.

Whether or not we build our lives into a home where God is welcomed and His Presence enjoyed will depend on whether we voluntarily lay the building blocks of our lives before Him. Believers who never experience the intimate friendship with God provided by Jesus have failed to understand such relationship isn't a given or a duty, but a privilege. We don't have to build our lives into a sanctuary for God. We get to, just as the people of Israel were told to bring voluntary contributions to build the temple "as their hearts moved them."

The Hebrew word for those tangible materials the Israelites contributed for the building of the temple is *terumah,* meaning "an offering for sacred use." Though believers do give tithes and offerings to support the Lord's work, the materials we bring to build a life in Him aren't all tangible. To build our lives into God's home, we bring Him the ongoing sacrifices of self. And just like the Israelites, our every offering of self is voluntary, by divine design.

For whoever wishes to save his life will lose it; but whoever loses his life for My sake will find it (Matthew 16:25 NASB).

God didn't violate our will before we came to faith, and He won't violate our will once we're His. We'll miss or discover the blessings of seeing our lives built into His dwelling place by one yielded choice on top of another, relinquishing our will to His.

Therefore I urge you, brethren, by the mercies of God, to present your bodies a living and holy sacrifice, acceptable to God, which is your spiritual service of worship (Romans 12:1 NASB).

Every day, all day, we're given opportunities to cling to our right to ourselves or concede everything we are in voluntary offerings to everything He is. It's our privilege to bring God our eyes, ears, words, desires, thoughts, actions, goals, priorities, and intentions, and these choices build our lives into His dwelling place where *He will meet with us,* where *He will speak to us.* Granted, that's not an exhaustive list. It's an idea of the materials within reach of us all that can hinder our walk with God or build Him a home in our nine-to-fives.

Example? If we resist our self-willed inclination to respond to a perceived offense our way and ask God to empower us instead to react His way, we bring Him a voluntary offering of our right to our self. The world may not come to a stand-still, and we may not hear angels' wings fill the room, but we have it on the authority of God's Word that He sees and receives this personal gift.

The sacrifices of God are a broken spirit; a broken and a contrite heart, O God, You will not despise (Psalm 51:17 NASB).

A broken spirit and contrite heart depict a yielded will, and a yielded will says, "He is God and I am not." What I'm about to say is so crucial, I find myself once again wishing we were sharing face-to-face: Jesus and the blood covenant He made with God on our behalf is the only reason these surrendered moments can build our lives into God's treasured home. It's critically important for us to recognize this truth, hold it dear, and never stop celebrating it.

Blood covenant? I know. We've mentioned it a couple of times, and it sounds deep. Brace yourself, we're going in.

Oh, the Blood

My sister Rhonda and my cousin Lisa were somewhere around ten years old the summer of our solemn ceremony. That would've made me a mature nine as we three stood in the backyard of our grandparents' house in Natchez, Mississippi, taking turns poking our fingers with a straight pin taken from Grandma Stone's sewing basket. One by one, our respective forefingers bore tiny dots of bright red blood. Step one accomplished, we pressed our fingers together to blend the blood and pronounce ourselves bound by a mysterious blood covenant. No doubt we had borrowed the idea from a Saturday-night Western. What we expected to gain from that blood sacrifice I've long since forgotten, if I ever knew.

I find the blood covenant Jesus struck with God on our behalf equally mystifying. What's more, I'm convinced experts with a slew of theology degrees also fall short of completely understanding what happened when God the Father and God the Son walked through their costly plan to redeem fallen man through Jesus's perfect blood sacrifice. Thankfully, none of us needs to fully comprehend the depth of this eternal mystery to put our trust in the gorgeously simple words of John 3:16: *For God so loved the world, that He gave His only begotten Son, that whosoever believes in Him shall not perish, but have eternal life.*

God made it possible for even the simplest of thinkers (that's me) to understand that trusting Jesus puts us right with God. So why are we talking about bloody sacrifices and something as ancient as the Ark of the Covenant? Because the more we know about this physical box where God made provision to dwell among His people, the more we'll grasp the forever favor we have with God through Jesus. And the more we understand this gift of access, the less prone we'll be to settle for status quo twenty-first century Christianity and the more courage we'll have to reach for the deep and wide life—the fullest measure of relationship Jesus provided us through the Cross. So let's look closer. It's time to peek inside and see what God instructed to be kept in this golden box.

God's Curious Keepsakes

Scripture tells us there were three items in the Ark: a jar holding manna, an almond branch, and the Ten Commandments.

Behind the second veil there was a tabernacle which is called the Holy of Holies, having a golden altar of incense and the ark of the covenant covered on all sides with gold, in which was a golden jar holding the manna, and Aaron's rod which budded, and the tablets of the covenant ... (Hebrews 9:3-5 NASB)

Warning. These three items record Israel's ugliest moments—ugly moments that we can relate to across the centuries. But once we see how Jesus redeemed them—both for the Israelites and for us—we'll be on shouting ground.

The first item stored in the Ark was a golden jar holding the manna God gave the children of Israel to eat in the wilderness (Exodus 16 and Numbers 21). Here's my Cliff's Notes version of that story:

God's people were complaining He had brought them into the wilderness to die, so He sent them angels' food. The Israelites ate the free bread until the novelty wore off and then said, "What else you got?" Or something like that.

It wasn't the first time mankind rejected God's promise of provision. (Hey again, Eve.) Nor was it the last. (Hi, Shellie.) The daily manna foreshadowed God's intention to send Jesus, the true Bread of Life, to earth. Man would reject God's provision for eternal life and crucify Him instead. (I told you this wouldn't be pretty.)

The second item in the Ark was Aaron's rod (see Numbers 17). Aaron was the first high priest appointed by God. He foreshadowed Jesus, the Great High Priest. And how did the people respond to Aaron's authority? They rejected his wisdom, just as they would one day reject the authority of Jesus. (Mirror, mirror, on the wall, this isn't looking good at all.)

That brings us to the third item God commissioned to be stored in the Ark, the tablets of the Covenant, also known as The Ten Commandments. These are the second set of commandments. Moses destroyed the first set in a righteous hissy fit at the sight of the people worshipping a golden calf, remember? They'd grown tired of waiting on Moses to return and deliver God's standard and had gone back to their own idolatrous ways of worshipping what they could see, taste, and touch.

To recap, per God's instructions, we have in the Ark a symbol of man rejecting God's provision, man rejecting the wisdom of His authority, and man rejecting the beauty of His commandments. If it sounds familiar, it's because we're looking at the Fall again, all wrapped up in one inglorious bundle of sin. Ugh. Why ever would God want these embarrassing keepsakes in this holiest of spaces, right below the seat where He promised to dwell?

Let's connect some dots. As we've already noted, this box was topped with a mercy seat, upon which the high priest applied the blood of an animal to atone for the sins of the people. With that applied blood, those mementos were covered before God's eyes! We've also established this golden lid as a replica of Heaven's true Mercy Seat. Today, the blood of Christ, God's perfect Lamb, rests on Heaven's Mercy Seat. Let's break it down further still.

Remember the manna? When God looks at Heaven's Mercy Seat, He doesn't see you and me rejecting His provision. He sees Jesus choosing to live on His Father's words, valuing them above anything the world offers.

But He answered and said, "It is written, 'Man shall not live on bread alone, but on every word that proceeds out of the mouth of God.'" (Matthew 4:4 NASB)

Jesus said to them, "My food is to do the will of Him who sent Me and to accomplish His work." (John 4:34 NASB)

Aaron's almond branch? Instead of God seeing man rejecting His authority, He sees Jesus perfectly submitting to it.

And he went a little beyond them, and fell on his face and prayed, saying, "My Father, if it be possible, let this cup pass from Me; yet, not as I will, but as you will." (Matthew 26:39 NASB)

Finally, see the Ten Commandments, broken and disregarded before God's eyes; they're covered by the blood of Jesus, too. Instead of seeing man rebel against His holy standard, God sees Jesus, the High Priest, perfectly obeying His commandments.

"But so that the world may know that I love the Father, I do exactly as the Father commanded Me." (John 14:31 NASB)

Christ's blood forever covering man's rejection of God's provision, His authority, and His commandments. No wonder God the Father loves the Son to infinity, right? This is where we tend to think *But I knew Jesus was perfect. What I don't understand is how His perfection can help me believe a holy God wants to set up house with unholy me when I fall so short of the Savior's perfection?*

We've officially arrived at the shouting ground! Let's soak in the glittering truth of the Gospel: All the favor Jesus has with the Father, the sum total of all that victory, the whole kit and caboodle of approval and blessings ascribed to His perfect life of obedience—Scripture says these belong to you, to me, and to all who believe. Mark it, star it, read it again and again.

But now apart from the Law the righteousness of God has been manifested, being witnessed by the Law and the Prophets, even the righteousness of God through faith in Jesus Christ for all who believe (Romans 3:20-22 NASB).

By this, love is perfected with us, so that we may have confidence in the day of judgment; because as He is, so are we in this world (1 John 4:17 NASB).

As He is, so are we in this world? This is what Jesus did when He reconciled us to the Father. He granted us His perfect, privileged standing. Forever.

Jesus makes it possible for us to live as He lived, in His Father's presence, enjoying God's favor—right now as you're reading these words and for all eternity. Here's how the writer of Hebrews explains it:

For Christ did not enter a holy place made with hands, a mere copy of the true one, but into heaven itself, now to appear in the presence of God for us; nor was it that He would offer Himself often, as the high priest enters the holy place year by year with blood that is not his own. Otherwise,

He would have needed to suffer often since the foundation of the world; but now once at the consummation of the ages He has been manifested to put away sin by the sacrifice of Himself (Hebrews 9:24-26 NASB).

Jesus, our High Priest, sprinkled His own sinless blood on Heaven's Mercy Seat once for all, forever atoning for man's sins and reconciling us to God. Our sins, gone. *Like it never even happened.*

We grasp so little of all we've inherited in Christ! It's like having the smartest phone ever and using it to check the time. There's so much more. I'm praying for us to have *"a spirit of wisdom and of revelation in the knowledge of Him. I pray that the eyes of your heart may be enlightened, so that you will know what is the hope of His calling, what are the riches of the glory of His inheritance in the saints"* (Ephesians 1:17 NASB).

I dare you to embrace this so much more with me. I hope I've whetted your appetite with the biographies of people who lived and loved God in a different way than those around them. God's Son has made such an above-average life available to all of us!

Which brings us back full-circle to a question we raised early in these pages: If we're fully forgiven and forever welcome, why do we allow ourselves to be cheated out of God's Presence? Why do we settle for the hope of eternal life later while we struggle to hold on and hold up in our own weak and exhausting efforts now?

We've addressed a couple of those answers, like the part our secular/sacred mentality plays in our fragmented relationship, but it's time we look at one of the most common traps the enemy lays for anyone who sets out to know God beyond their initial salvation. I know this one well, and I believe it's one of his more successful snares. Meet me in the next chapter. I'll begin by telling you a story . . .

Questions for Group Study or Private Reflection

1. What is the important distinction Shellie makes about the building materials of the Old Testament tabernacle?

2. How does that answer correspond to our hope of building our lives into a place where God is pleased to dwell?
3. Compose a short prayer expressing your gratitude to Jesus for all He fulfilled that we might enjoy His favor. Be intentional about mentioning the three items in the Ark.

Chapter Thirteen

The God Who Got in Our Crib

*"You cannot make yourself different.
Jesus came to give you a new heart, a new spirit, a new mind,
and a new body. Let him transform you by his love
and so enable you to receive his affection in your whole being."*

HENRI NOUWEN

I had no sooner typed that line about allowing ourselves to be cheated out of God's company than I imagined my editor telling me I'd need to explain both what I meant by that and my reasons for saying it. Again, experience has taught me to trust the way editors think, so I decided to conduct an impromptu poll among my Christian friends to test my theory.

Grabbing my handy smart phone, I sent an informal text message to a couple dozen believers, young and old, male and female. A few were in the ministry, most were not.

I give you the actual text I composed that afternoon, sans the random emoticons I interspersed thereabouts because I'm an emoticon addict.

Hi, friends! This is not a test. I'm asking a ton of people this question today. It's research for a book I'm working on, but I promise not to use your names. Oh, and I'm copying and pasting individually instead of using a group text to protect your privacy. Please respond as transparently, and honestly as possible. You can use one word or a hundred. I realize I may have caught you at a busy time. I won't be trying to engage you in an ongoing text conversation other than to say thank you for answering. Tomboy honor! So, here's my question:

Do you live with a sense that God is pleased with you?

Over the next few hours, their responses trickled in, and my heart began to ache. A clear majority of the good, honest, Jesus-loving, church-going people I polled confessed that while they knew theologically God loved them, they didn't live with the sense He was pleased with them. Worse still, most suspected they disappointed God more often than they pleased Him.

This wasn't shocking. It largely confirmed my suspicions, but as I continued to scan their feedback, a theme began to develop in their answers that rocked me. Thoroughly. I wouldn't have been surprised had they cited their behavior as the basis for God's supposed displeasure, what they were doing right or wrong—and indeed, a few did respond that way. However, the larger majority credited one common reason for His displeasure, and it was one I didn't see coming.

They felt sure they disappointed God by not spending more time with Him.

I don't know if that grabs you, but it was sobering news for someone writing a book tracing God's desire to be with us, all in hopes of unsettling our status-quo faith and lighting a passion in us to respond to His timeless passion. But there it was, a tally of candid responses presenting that recurring question, begging to be answered.

If we know God wants to be a part of our day-to-day lives, why do we keep Him shut out?

No doubt that question has a ton of answers. In the remaining pages, we'll explore some of the hindrances I've experienced and outline ways to get past them.

We hinted at my first theory in earlier chapters, so we won't spend much time there. Basically, we're not convinced our getting-up, lying-down, walking-around lives hold much pleasure for God. So we wait until we're in our disciplined devotionals and sanctified services to try to engage with Him. And yet God is repeatedly pictured in His Word as throwing a party and inviting His guests to laugh, linger, and enjoy themselves. (Think about the prodigal son's homecoming party.)

If God didn't sanction the entire human experience, He wouldn't have set us in families and designed us for work and play, activity and rest, eating and sleeping. All of life is His invention. Can these things become twisted and out of proportion in our lives? Sure. But if they do, the fault lies with us, not in their divine design. So, yes, the secular/sacred mindset is at play, but we're about to discover another reason we don't enjoy what Christ has made available.

Even now, as I picture the believers who responded to my poll, it hurts to know so many of them doubt their place in God's affections. If their estrangement hurts me, I can't imagine how it grieves the Lover of our souls Who so longed to redeem us that He came as one of us to reunite all of us. God provided Himself a dwelling place in our lives, and it's not a Sunday place or a devotional space for super saints. He joins us to rescue us.

The great Apostle Paul described it this way: *God was in Christ reconciling the world to Himself, not counting their trespasses against them* ... (2 Corinthians 5:19 NASB)

I remember my daughter-in-law Carey telling me about something that happened in the middle of a long line of sleepless nights. Carey had one leg hoisted over the side of Weston the Wonder Boy's baby bed to climb into it with him when common sense prevailed. The tired mama conceded. As desperate as she was to console her son so the two of them could catch some Z's, they simply weren't going to fit in those close quarters. Granted, double-bunking in Weston's crib wasn't Plan A, or B, or C, but having sick kids—Weston's sisters were also under the weather—can lead a sleep-deprived parent to consider extreme measures.

I resemble that. Long years ago, my own toddlers came down with miserable cases of the chicken pox simultaneously. Sores covered their bodies and invaded their eyes, ears, and throats. Their pediatrician prescribed oatmeal baths to ease their discomfort, and it worked at first. But as relief got harder to come by, the baths began losing their appeal. Team Tomlinson was in trouble.

The troops were growing increasingly miserable, and their exhausted leader was becoming ever more desperate. Which accounts for the fond memory I have of sitting in a late-night oatmeal bath with two despondent toddlers because they were convinced my presence would make it all better, and Lord knows our tribe needed some relief.

Carey and I were commiserating and laughing over these stories the morning after her crib adventure, via text, when I had the sweetest of thoughts. I sent her a follow-up message and our laughter turned into praise.

"Hey, Carey," I typed. "Jesus got in our oatmeal bath with us! He got in our crib!"

Of course, what Jesus did for us goes far beyond those loving parental gestures. We were lost, alone, and without hope in this world, doomed without Him. The Son of God joined us to rescue us. Being fully man, He gets us. Being fully God, He redeems us.

Let's turn our attention to the Apostle John. We can learn so much from him about learning to live in the love of God.

Jesus Loves Me, This I Know

If John had a soapbox, it was about abiding in God's love. But "abiding" sounds so theological, and that can be intimidating. Another way to think about abiding is the simple idea of dwelling and remaining. Not coming and going, not visiting, but continuing, in one place. John returned to the foundational truth of being loved by God throughout his writings. If we'll listen, his message can rescue us from our self-imposed exiles from God's presence.

Much has been made of John's penchant for describing himself as "the one whom God loves." It tickles me, too. I wish John had been on our group text. It would've been interesting to hear his response, but what I want to know is this: Why was John so secure in his relationship with God? Why could he proclaim with confidence, *"We have come to know and have believed the love which God has for us"* (1 John 4:16 NASB)?

We'd all like to feel as loved by God as John did. Right? We hear the admonition to love God with all our heart, mind, and soul, and we start trying to gin up some passion, hoping to kick-start the type of relationship John enjoys. We try our best to generate love toward God because we know we should love Him. But John knew something far better! John knew we can only love God because God loves us.

We love, because He first loved us (1 John 4:19 NASB).

You might be thinking, *Whatever, Shellie, we know that, too.*

I agree. At least we know it when we first come to faith in Christ. But what happens when we discover there's plenty of the old us left in the new us? How do we live in God's ever-steady love when we're painfully aware our passion for Him ebbs and flows?

John had the answer. He didn't ground his confidence in his love for God but in God's love for him. John nurtured a growing, enduring love for God by feeding on His extravagant, unearned, and ongoing affection for him. John gave more than mental assent to the truth of God's love. He feasted on it until it became his experience. He understood holy love is sustained where holy love begins. Follow John every time he climbs up on his soapbox, and you'll see him forever teaching God loves first, and God loves best.

For instance, in this same passage of 1 John, the apostle says building our faith on God's love for us does two incredible things:

It gives us great confidence on the Day of Judgment, and it causes us to love others.

We have come to know and have believed the love which God has for us. God is love, and the one who abides in love abides in God, and God abides in him. By this, love is perfected with us, so that we may have confidence in the day of judgment; because as He is, so also are we in this world. There is no fear in love; but perfect love casts out fear, because fear involves punishment, and the who one fears is not perfected in love . . . (1 John 4:16-19 NASB)

There's that fear again—fear of judgment, of not measuring up. Now, that's interesting. Remember my informal poll and how the majority felt God wasn't pleased with them because they didn't spend enough time with Him? Don't miss the connection. *If we don't live shoring our shaky selves up on the eternal, rock-solid, never-changing love of God, we will live feeling like we're falling short of God's requirements and He is tolerating us—at best.* It's flawed thinking, but it's our default position, and it's not conducive to divine intimacy.

Feasting on God's love refutes our insecurities and wrecks the persistent whispers of our enemy. Meditating on the truth of God's Word draws us to Him over and again. This is what John understood. He knew living in celebration of God's love for us causes our love for Him to respond as naturally and easily as a seed responds to rain or a flower to the sun.

And don't say you don't know how to meditate. We're all good at thinking the wrong thoughts to death. Our challenge is to retrain ourselves to think long and hard on the *right* ones. Meditating is simply thinking about something and thinking about it again.

The more we remind ourselves of God's love, shown to us in the gift of Jesus, who permanently reconciled us and brought us into His forever favor, cleansed now, cleansed later—the more we delight in such unmerited status, the more encouraged we become to draw nearer still. And that ever-present guilt we have about not spending enough time with Him? It falls away because we can no longer get enough of His friendship. Instead of spending time with God out of a warped sense of duty, trying to please Him with our presence, we find ourselves longing for more of His.

Soul Therapy

John had a co-worker named Jude, the brother of Jesus, who taught this same valuable lesson of shoring ourselves up in God's love. Most scholars agree Jude is the half-brother of Jesus, and like his brother James, he didn't come to faith in Christ until after Jesus's death and resurrection.

Unlike John, Jude was a man of few words. He wrote one chapter with twenty-five verses. (I take that long just to set up a story, but I digress.)

In the twenty-first verse of his only chapter, Jude encouraged his readers to keep themselves in the love of God. Now, surely Jude can't be saying it's up to us to maintain our place in God's love. This One who loves us and has pledged never to leave us or forsake us! No, indeed. (Other translations read "remain" in His love.)

Jude is recommending the same thing as John—continually celebrating our place in God's affections. For ongoing soul therapy, I suggest we take in the following words Jesus spoke to His followers and repeat them to ourselves every day.

"In that day you will ask in My name, and I do not say to you that I will request of the Father on your behalf; for the Father Himself loves you, because you have loved Me, and have believed that I came forth from the Father." (John 16:26-27 NASB)

Sweet solace. The Father loves us because we believe Jesus came from Him.

But why would Jude and John both think we need to be constantly reminded of God's love? Maybe because trusting Jesus doesn't give us spiritual amnesia? Maybe because I can hide from you and you can hide from me, but we can't hide from ourselves, and we know we can't hide who we really are from God. He knows there are many days when we fall more than we follow, and we know He knows.

And if it's not enough for us to live beating ourselves up, we also wake up under the assault of an enemy bent on trapping us in the muck of ourselves. Satan schemes to make us feel guilty for not measuring up, and if that doesn't work, he'll work to make us feel superior, prideful, and judgmental. Whichever shoe fits is the one he'll try to force on our human feet, all to keep us out of the transforming presence of God. This is why it's crucially important for us to shore up our faith on God's love.

Because of the Lord's great love we are not consumed, for his compassions never fail. They are new every morning; great is your faithfulness (Lamentations 3:22–23 NIV).

We need to keep reminding ourselves of God's unfailing love for us, despite all we know about ourselves, because God's love is like none we experience on earth. We know the type of love that gets its fill of our failures and says, "That's enough, I'm done." But God's love knows no limits. In the words of one of my favorite worship songs by Jesus Culture, "Your love never fails, never gives up, never runs out on me."

By continuing to feast on God's love, we begin to build a sweet confidence in the most secure relationship we could hope for or imagine. We begin to grasp the marvelous truth. God not only loved enough to rescue us, He loves us enough to finish what He has begun, to stay with us until the job is done. It's astounding love, and feeding on it breeds humility, gratitude, and an eagerness for more.

To know this joy, we must let ourselves believe God finds joy in the process we see as a hot mess and build our lives on this sweet truth. We're His beloved, today. He's not waiting in Heaven to stamp us with His divine approval once our transformation is complete.

Ode to the Remodel

My man and I have just finished making over our master bathroom. Over the years, I've noticed we go through three stages in almost every home-improvement job we tackle: let's do it; why on earth are we doing it?; and praise God Almighty, we did it!

For a while, it seemed we'd never get out of Stage Two on this one. It was hard to remember why we were doing it when mortar dust started blanketing everything in sight, despite the plastic sheeting that was supposed to contain it to one room, but our enthusiasm took a direct hit the day the water pipe busted. Water plus mortar equals mud.

To double the fun, it was my speaking and traveling season. I was meeting myself coming and going during those long weeks of remodeling, and my beloved hubby, along with our contractor, was asking me questions over the phone that were way above my pay grade. (That's okay. I may have asked Mr. Contractor a few questions during that long season, too. Like, "Hey Ronnie, which of these necklaces do you like with this outfit?")

And yet, glory hallelujah, Stage Three finally arrived. We did it! Stage Two may have been hard, but we love Stage Three. When we look at it now, we're incredibly pleased with what we see.

As believers, you and I are kind of like Stage Two—works in progress. And yes, we're a major home-improvement job, but God the Father and God the Son counted the cost, paid the bill in full, and together they're enjoying the process of renovating our lives. Even as Jesus completes the good work He began in us, He and His Father are pleased with what they see. Oh, feast here.

Phil and I were pleased once our remodel was finished, but Jesus is pleased to live with you and me in the messy middle of our renovation! Is He pleased with our every action? That answer should be obvious, but we'll leave the biblical equivalent of a pink elephant here if we don't address it.

Throughout the church age, there's been often-repeated concern: *Be careful in teaching on grace and God's willingness to forgive again and again lest you encourage people to think they can give in to the desires of the flesh, live any way they choose, and still be secure in their faith.*

I don't necessarily disagree, but I'm not speaking to those looking for permission to live a sloppy Christian life. I've got this conviction that says if you want to be rebellious and disobedient, you will be.

But if you're reading these words, I believe you want what I want—to know how to stop doing what we don't want to do, start doing what we do want to do, and experience the full measure of our salvation. Such a life comes only out of deep realization that we are, right now, righteous in God's sight through our faith in Jesus's great sacrifice. Full conviction of our wholly undeserved place in God's favor produces ongoing humility and encourages grateful communion. We want to live for Him because He died for us. Savoring the full extent of His gift to us, woven with the goal of living to know one more thing about Him to add to our growing treasure—this is what changes moments, moods, and men.

So, no, God isn't pleased with our disobedience, but our Father can separate who we are from what we do. We're fallible parents, and yet we understand this when it relates to our own children. Am I right?

A few years ago, our immediate family enjoyed a delicious meal together. We adults were washing up the dishes when my son's middle child wandered through the kitchen in different clothes than she had been wearing when they arrived. Her parents exchanged glances. Carlisle had been potty trained for quite a while, but she was currently regressing. She'd get busy playing, wait too long, and, well, there you go. (Pun intended.)

This doting grandmother understands accidents happen. Her parents do, too, but they're tasked with helping their girl to remember. They knew Carlisle had found the extra set of little girl's clothes in the laundry room, and they knew why she'd pulled a switcheroo. Phillip stopped his little one in her tracks. "Carlisle Mae," he said. "Did you change clothes?"

Carlisle's attempt to disarm her daddy with a cheesy grin was unsuccessful. The clock was ticking.

"Carlisle," Philip repeated. "Did you wet your pants?"

Carlisle is the owner of a thousand expressions, and she keeps us on our toes. Her well-thought-out response didn't permanently put off her moment of reckoning, but every one of us had to turn around and compose ourselves when she replied, "Maybe ..."

Isn't this how most of us come to the subject of obedience? Tell me how bad the repercussions will be, and I'll tell you what I have or haven't done. That is religion's version of obedience. Jesus turned the whole subject upside down when He died so He could live in us and empower us to obey. The more we abide in Him and marinate in His amazing love, the more what we do responds to who He purposed us to be. Crazy cool. God looks upon us with pleasure when we are in Christ Jesus. Together they celebrate what Jesus announced on the cross, "It is finished!" (John 19:30)

Hear them now, looking at us in the middle of our renovation (the doctrinal word is "sanctification"), surveying the work of the Cross, and announcing with joy, "We did it!"

This is the reality of Jesus; He is our everything.

He is our meeting place between God and man, and He is the Holy One beyond the veil.

He is the High priest who brought the blood sacrifice and the sacrifice atoning for the sins of the people.

He is the altar where the sacrifice was brought, and He is the sacrifice.

Jesus is the mercy seat affixed on the golden ark and the Presence dwelling there.

Everything. Jesus is all in all. The very Holy of Holies living in us, meant to walk through this life with us.

Remember when we noted the Ark's intentionally designed portability? God instructed the Israelites to equip the golden box that served as meeting place between God and men with poles and rings so they could carry it about. He didn't want to come and go in the lives of the children of Israel, and He doesn't want to come and go in ours. He didn't want to be worshipped only on their holy days, and He has no interest in being our Sunday-morning God. He wanted them to know what it was to live, work, and play in His presence, and He wants this for us.

God won't drag us into the deep and wide, and we can't find it by trying harder to do better. That's religion, man meeting the bar man sets so man feels good about man. Living life with Christ is as far from such a religious system built on rule-keeping as the east is from the west.

Looking to Jesus for salvation is to inherit eternal life. To look again, and again, to live looking at Him instead of us—this is what the Bible calls "beholding" Him. And it's the secret of a life being molded by Christ! If we'll quit plotting our progress and fix our eyes on Jesus, He'll do the heavy lifting of making us over into His image.

"Beholding," you might say. "What an ancient word."

You're right, and I know you have questions. *Behold how, when, where?* We'll get to them. Right now, we have a few more traps to expose that can keep us from a life of beholding.

Questions for Group Study or Private Reflection

1. How would you have answered Shellie's text?
2. What did the Apostle John understand about how to sustain his love toward God?
3. Why does Shellie suggest we need to continually shore ourselves up on the foundation of God's love for us?

Chapter Fourteen

. . . . .

Jesus, the Open Door

"The Christian life starts with grace, it must continue with grace, it ends with grace. Grace wondrous grace."

—MARTYN LLOYD-JONES

I spotted it during my morning's extreme makeover. No. Stinking. Way. I leaned in closer and looked again. Surely not. I grabbed my magnifying mirror, thinking there was no way I was seeing what I thought I was seeing, but I was. A single black hair and it was growing beneath my bottom lip. Beneath my bottom *lip*, y'all!

I'm not talking about a chin hair. (If you're female and of a certain age, you're already doing something about those, and if you aren't, prepare yourself, time waits for no one.) This wasn't that. I'm talking about a black hair the length of my eyelashes, growing on my face beneath my bottom lip, right in front of God and everybody. While you're processing, consider this. I was just coming off a long series of back-to-back traveling weekends, where I'd spoken to a variety of audiences in several cities. Somebody pass Mama the smelling salts.

I grabbed a pair of tweezers and removed the hairy offender faster than quick while I tried not to think about how many people might have seen the thing. Afterward, I called my girlfriends for comfort. That was a fail.

"You've got yourself a wisdom patch," the first one said, after she caught her breath from laughing like a maniac. "That's what they call that little patch of hair beneath a man's lip."

I hung up on her.

One of my younger friends disagreed. "Nope," she said. "It's called a soul patch."

Thanks for nothing, Miss Thang.

Wisdom patch, soul patch—they both missed the point. I wanted to know why no one had been kind enough to give me a heads-up. As far as I know, I don't look like the type of woman who would be growing a soul patch beneath her bottom lip on purpose.

By the way, if there are any male people reading this, I figure you're getting a chuckle out of my embarrassing facial hair episode. I'm okay with that, too. I really do think life is better when you're laughing. But keep in mind, y'all have your own issues. We used to think you were losing your hair. We now realize it's changing directions and growing back out of your ears and nose, kind of like a reverse chia pet.

But back to my own unfortunate discovery. As embarrassing as it was, it did explain some things. Back in the day, I'd see an older lady with stray hairs growing in curious places on her face and I'd think to myself, *Bless her heart. Why doesn't she pluck that?* Now I know why. If we were all in the same room, I'd make eye contact with a younger woman for this next revelation: She couldn't see it! For Heaven's sake, help a girl out.

That's what I'm hoping to do about the hindrances that keep believers from enjoying Jesus.

I have two big reasons for throwing in that humor break at my own expense. First, I want to make sure there is zero pretense between us. I'm journeying right along with you in the real world. And second, because while the things that once kept me from enjoying God's day-to-day presence may seem obvious now, that was not always the case, and I can't help believing my experiences can help someone else.

I've spent so much time in my life spinning in circles, trying to earn what was already mine in Christ Jesus. If I let myself, I could bemoan it all as wasted time, but I refuse to live there. If my story with God can help you connect to Him, if by standing on my shoulders you can get closer to Heaven faster, it's all valuable, and every moment redeemed.

I want to whet your appetites with the possibilities of a deep and wide life in Christ. The promise of the Gospel is that every single one of us can enjoy intimacy with God through Christ. We can all come to a place where we crave God's Word instead of resigning ourselves to reading it when we can because we know we should. Every single one of us can come to love and live on prayer instead of going through the motions out of dry commitment. This is our birthright.

The Open Door

I woke up in my daughter's guestroom in Houston, Texas, with a phrase on my mind: *There's a door standing open …* We were enjoying the Thanksgiving holiday as a family. All five of my grandchildren were in the house, and I was relishing having them all together, so I tucked the words from Scripture in my heart for safe keeping. It was later, driving home to northeast Louisiana with my husband, that I began searching them out and listening for why the Lord brought it to my mind. The full sentence comes from Revelation 4:1: *After this I looked, and there before me was a door standing open in heaven* (NIV).

I suspect everyone reading this will know the identity of this door standing open in Heaven, but let's go to the gospel of John and establish it. Jesus said, *"I am the door; if anyone enters through Me, he will be saved, and will go in and out and find pasture."* (John 10:9 NASB)

Our invitation is to come to Jesus for eternal life.

Our challenge is to keep coming to Him for abundant life.

Have you settled somewhere between those two? You're not alone, and that's not a good thing.

I don't know what's more tragic, that this Door of nourishment and fellowship is undervalued and neglected by unbelievers or by believers! *Believers neglecting the Door, Shellie?* Yes. Our dry faith rats us out, and the Word testifies to our malnutrition.

John sees this Door in Revelation 4:1 after hearing Jesus speak to the seven churches in the preceding two chapters. Those addresses contain a record of grievances Jesus has with the church. Not the world, my friends, the *church*. Immediately following that discourse, we find Jesus giving the solution for their sins and indifference here in Revelation 4:1; the cure He prescribes is Himself, *the Door standing open in Heaven.*

It's painful to hear Jesus calling out the churches because, unfortunately, we can identify with them. And though we all need to confess where our sin and indifference mirrors theirs, I see another reason why we don't make effective use of the open Door, and that's where I want to camp in this chapter. I don't know how to cushion this, so I'll just say it.

I'm convinced we're ignorant of how to go about enjoying what is ours in Jesus. I have been, and in many ways still am, even though He has stirred in me a taste for His presence that keeps me running back for more.

How to come in and out of this Door that stands open in Heaven shouldn't be a secret, but both my personal experience and my years in women's ministry convince me it remains a mystery in the lives of far too many believers. We simply don't know how to live in the privileges Jesus has granted us. We know it's "all grace" that saves us, but we tend to apply truth to our eternal position in Christ without learning how to apply it to our daily life in Christ. We struggle to understand Jesus is our access to God when we come to believe and thereafter as we make our way to our forever home.

As I've confessed half a dozen times, I've been super-slow in learning how to use the Door that stands open in Heaven. It's why I now live to help others find their way there.

I want to share with you three biblically based habits that come straight out of my own experience in hopes of helping you learn to use the Door. These tools are not definitive, but I'm confident in this guarantee. If you use them, they'll help you embrace the life you were born to live, too!

For starters, we must learn to relate to God on the sure ground of the Cross, alone. That's our first heart habit.

What does that look like? Well, it's not memorizing that statement or any other combination of words. It refers to what the Apostle John taught us about learning to remind ourselves of God's love. It's a constant recognition of our need of Jesus every single time we approach God. It's celebrating His finished work as our access to God, not our most recent performance, not our present attitude or circumstance, and not our best intentions. It's Jesus, the Open Door.

I've learned to live celebrating the truth that I'm forgiven, accepted, and loved when I feel like it—and when I don't. I've discovered the power of reminding ourselves Jesus not only met the bar for us, He obliterated the measuring stick. I delight in reminding myself I'm not poked and prodded and scrutinized for admission at the Door. I'm warmly welcomed and fully received through Christ Jesus.

HEART HABIT #1: Learn to relate to God through the Cross of Christ, alone.

If you've ever tried to develop a prayer life, you'll recognize the follow scenario. One day, it feels like God is near and listening. Glorious, holy moments—if only you could hold onto them forever. Perhaps it was during your own devotional time, or maybe it was during a worship service with other believers. Either way, it was good, exceptionally good, until the next time you knelt to pray or lifted your eyes toward Heaven and got nothing, zero, nada. As much as you stammered and stuttered and reached for words, your mind wandered, your coldness of heart embarrassed you, and the most unfaithful thoughts and doubts seemed to rise out of your own spirit! Anybody?

I'll go first. Again. I don't mind. Surely, by now, you've figured out I'm not writing from a place of having arrived.

I used to deal with the ugly of me by trying harder to focus better and pray more fervently. For Heaven's sake, I'd even try to remember what song we were singing, what was being preached, or what devotional I was reading the last time I got all the feels. If none of that worked, I'd search my heart for something, anything, to confess. Just laying it out here, folks. That's dry bones and unfulfilling religion, and it stinketh to the high heavens. We talk of the fight of faith but fail to realize the greatest fight is about learning to rest in Jesus. Our most important work? To quit working.

Jesus answered, "The work of God is this: to believe in the one he has sent." (John 6:29 NASB)

Jesus says *believing* is our work. We like the sound of that, but we struggle to actually do it. The truth wiggles out of our grasp because believing seems too easy when we're broken and all around us we see people who need healing, reconciling, rescuing, reforming, reclaiming, and restoring. Believing that our work is believing feels like a cop-out, so we create courses to complete and stairs to run and ladders to climb and bars to reach while the unflinching Word stands in our midst repeating His eternal claim.

Our work is to believe Him, for when we believe Him, we trust Him; and when we trust Him, we live before Him; and when we live before Him, we start changing. The fixing begins in us and moves to those nearest us, and we become the hope we don't see, all because we dared to believe and keep believing.

To know the full joy of our salvation, we must learn to run to God through the Door that is Jesus when we're tempted and doubting and run to God through the Door that is Jesus when we're peaceful and trusting. Are you seeing the theme? All Jesus. All the time.

I want to cement this with an illustration I hope stays with you long after you close this book.

Fighting for Our Lives

When my grands spend the night, I tuck them into bed in a guest room down our back hall. They've learned that come the next morning, they'll find me in the great room with my Bible and my coffee. As soon as their little eyes open, they are bent on one destination—Keggie and her chair. Down the hall they come.

Let me tell you what they don't do when they reach the great room door. They don't peek around the corner to try to gauge my mood. They don't try to decide if they should close the distance quickly or if they should tiptoe toward me. They don't stand there wondering if they should sing loud or low, fast or slow. They don't wonder if Keggie is going to be happy to see them or if she is upset because they ate the candy she told them not to eat the day before, and they don't worry about whether they broke something she told them not to touch.

Oh, no, ma'am! They round the corner without breaking stride! Hopefully, I've heard them coming and put my coffee down because once they get close to my chair, they launch themselves at me. I catch them, and we snuggle, giggle, and talk. And yes, I may have a talk with them about the hidden candy or the broken vase. Or I might tell them what we're going to do that day and what I expect of them. Direction, correction, or affection—it all comes out of intimacy and fellowship.

This is the privilege of relationship granted us in Christ Jesus. Nothing in us can earn it, and nothing in us can keep it. But because this grace-soaked Gospel seems to us too good to be true in the face of what we know about ourselves, it behooves us to live reminding ourselves over and again that our access to God comes through Jesus, the Door. I wasn't exaggerating when I said this *is* the fight of our spiritual lives. If we don't fight to rest in what Jesus has done and is doing, we'll fall back into our old efforts to sustain and obtain what we didn't begin and can't finish! Jesus gives us new life, and we must have Jesus to live it. Jesus, faith's rest.

I'm not suggesting we change our speech patterns in prayer. I'm advocating the power of always positioning and repositioning our hearts with this one understanding, that I forever approach Father God through Christ Jesus. In this light, instead of closing my prayers in Jesus's name, I've begun opening them in His name. Not to get my words right, but to make sure my heart is right.

But Shellie, are you saying I can't ever come to God in prayer without verbally or mentally acknowledging that I'm coming through Jesus? Are you saying I can't just start praising God and trusting that He will hear me? Oh, of course you can, and of course He does.

I'm saying every time we go to Him, we are heard because of Jesus, and we pay a tragic cost when we lose sight of this. There's untold reward in reminding ourselves He is the Door, lest we find ourselves entangled in our own efforts and doing seventy-five spiritual pushups to be heard. Blessed are the try-harders who learn to guzzle grace in this dry and thirsty land.

This is what I'm telling you. My own heart that now lives hungry for Jesus can still go from cold to hot and hot to cold faster than you can say quick. Does this grieve me? Sure, it does! I don't want to be lukewarm when my Jesus is on fire. My humanness gives my enemy countless opportunities to wedge between me and the One my soul loves unless I remind myself to wrench my eyes from my work-in-progress self and begin celebrating Christ Jesus. Again. This habit is opening the door of fellowship for me beyond my wildest imaginations.

These days, when I catch myself searching for the right spiritual formula because God feels distant or analyzing myself ad nauseum, I throw on the brakes and run for the Door that is Jesus my Lord. I ask His Spirit to stir my lukewarm heart into a flame. As a matter of fact, I've discovered my vital need of asking Him to help me pray every single time I reach for Him and not just when He feels distant.

I can no more pray without the help of the Holy Spirit than I can obey without His help, speak without His help, or serve without His help! Owning my perennial need has become my ongoing strength. I stand on naked faith in the Cross of Christ and remind myself that through Jesus, I'm in God's favor forever.

But I said when I *catch* myself. You saw that? It's present tense. As I've confessed, I'm not beyond getting stuck in the muck of me, but I've found that when I live asking the Holy Spirit to alert me to my wrong thinking, He is faithful to do precisely that, and those times are growing fewer and further apart. He'll do this for you, too.

The Spirit of God is ever willing to blow on the fire He started in our hearts, but we must quit trying to stir our lagging passion by working up repentance or charting our obedience. One of the greatest discoveries of our believing lives is when we realize the hope for our passionless, disjointed, hit-and-miss faith is found in the same One Who gave us the first measure! Oh, glory.

Have you learned to cry out of your dry heart for more passion for His Word, His Presence, His will? Try it, and get back to me when you're incredulous at what He is doing in you. We'll celebrate together!

Teach me your way, Lord, that I may rely on your faithfulness; give me an undivided heart, that I may fear your name. I will praise you, Lord my God, with all my heart; I will glorify your name forever (Psalm 86:11-12 NASB).

Questions for Group Study or Private Reflection

1. Shellie recommends worshipping Jesus early, often, and always as a heart habit that develops a strong prayer life. Find a Scripture in the Bible that would support this.
2. Shellie uses the expression "Run for the Door." What does that mean to you?
3. What does Jesus define as the work of God in John 6:29? How is this different than what we tend to think of as the work of God?

Chapter Fifteen

. . . . .

Dying to Live

"When we come to the end of ourselves,
we come to the beginning of God."

—Billy Graham

There's a white, furry, heart-shaped rug in our master bedroom, on my side of the bed. No one sees it from the door, so for the most part, only God and I know it's there. (Oh, and now y'all do, but you'll sleep and forget, right?)

The rug was a gift from my bestie. She saw it and knew it would be a perfect gift. Red's traveled many a ministry mile with me, and bless her own dear soul, she's heard me speak more than anyone on the planet should have to other than Jesus. The girl needs a crown for that alone.

Red knows my strengths, my weaknesses, and my routines, and she's well acquainted with my crazy. It's a close match to her own. (You can experience our matching crazy all over social media, but don't say you weren't warned.) She also knows about my fondness for hearts. I've been collecting them in every size and shape imaginable for years, ever since I started asking Jesus to take the broken want-to

161

of this heart that didn't know how to love Him and turn it into His happy place.

Red knows about my habit of sliding out of bed to my knees and why I formed it. She knows I'll be there for a few seconds, at the most. She knows it isn't my prayer time, just a bare moment of intentional yielding. It's me saying, "Boss me, today, Jesus. I surrender me, again."

Of course, Red can't always travel with me. She has plenty of obligations that keep her at home. But once, I was coming off a long ministry weekend where I had been traveling many miles with just me, myself, and Jesus, when Red surprised me with her gift. My spirit was full, but the flesh was weary and needing a nap when Red went with the "close your eyes I've got something for you" thing. I complied, and when I opened my eyes, there stood my longtime buddy grinning like a crazy person and holding that furry, white, heart-shaped rug. That rug now marks the spot of my daily dying, and I love it. (Thanks, Red!)

I don't write about my rug to convince you to take up the habit of going to your knees before you take to your feet. I realize some of you have physical limitations that hinder you from slipping to the floor in the morning. But I do write to double-dog dare you to adopt the heart habit of ignoring yourself, surrendering everything you are to everything He is, yield to Him all day, and then yield again tomorrow and the day after that. Oh, and start early, like as soon as your eyes open. Why? Because Jesus will be our everything or our nothing today, but He refuses to be our side hustle. Because whatever our day holds, nothing in it can compare to a millisecond of His Presence, and we must die to ourselves to live in Him. Having enough Jesus to think you're making it to Heaven will never be enough Jesus for us once we begin to realize our constant need of a Savior and learn to nourish ourselves in His Presence, walking nearer still.

Then he said to them all: "Whoever wants to be my disciple must deny themselves and take up their cross daily and follow me. For whoever wants to save their life will lose it, but whoever loses their life for me will save it." (Luke 9:23-24 NASB, emphasis mine)

Daily. Underline that word. Star it. Jot it on a sticky note.

The biggest hindrance we have to finding the deep and wide life with Jesus we're looking for stares back at us in the bathroom mirror every morning. It's us.

Daily fellowship requires daily surrender, and we need to have that settled before the world starts crowding in with countless opportunities to choose our will or yield to God's. In yielding our will, we must learn to include both the present moment and our right to the one down the road. Our temptation is to leave ourselves secret "wiggle" room in our thinking to act, say, and do what we please over X, Y, or Z, if we decide we've gotten a belly full. It may not be a conscious decision, but reserving some measure of us for ourselves is a pending will, not a yielded will.

Absolute surrender refuses to reserve an out by trusting Jesus to empower our obedience in the future, just as He saved us in the past, and just as HE is strengthening us in the present. It's a deeper consecration, it brings a fuller joy, and it's our second heart habit. Living as the bossed with Jesus as the boss.

Side story: I got an email once from a well-meaning lady who had heard me speak and wanted me to know she didn't approve of my using language about Jesus bossing me. She thought it was sacrilegious. I meant no disrespect then, and I mean none now. When I ask Jesus to boss me, I'm basically confessing what God and I both know. My flesh is going to want to rule the day, but my desire is to live dying to self and yielding to Jesus. I'm saying I aim to ignore my me monster, and I'm acknowledging I'll need His indwelling help!

Yes, I have a me monster. Brace yourself. You do, too.

HEART HABIT #2: Ignore your me monster.

This past Christmas season, my daughter and her family were visiting from Houston. Sunday morning found them at church with us, along with my son and his family who live in our hometown and regularly worship with us there.

Our pastor's wife teaches our children's church, and she takes the commitment seriously. Kelly defines the word "dependable," and it's rare for her to miss a service. And yet, that Sunday morning, an announcement was made that Kelly was ill and the kids were going to be in big service with the adults. This would've been fine had I not felt a nudge to fill in for her. The pull grew stronger as I watched the sanctuary fill up with young parents and their accompanying balls of pure energy. Spare the writing on the wall. This was a no-brainer. Thankfully, another grandmother was feeling the same call.

Sometime later, the two of us were leading the kids in a very impromptu conversation about what happened in the Garden of Eden after watching an animated movie on the subject.

My grandson Connor sat in front of me as I led the discussion. Connor is seven, the next to youngest of our five grands. He has big, gorgeous brown eyes and they were glued on mine.

Here's what you need to know about Connor. He is personality plus! Connor has a rubber face with a thousand expressions and a heart as big as Texas. He is also as headstrong as they come. My daughter, Jessica, and I had been praying and believing for the day when Connor would surrender that strong will to God, but we couldn't have known He was about to begin answering those prayers.

That morning, our conversation in children's church took a most unusual turn—at least for the average age of those present. To be sure, I can't remember how we got there. All I know is, I was telling the kids it wasn't all about the apple. It was about Eve wanting to do what she wanted to do instead of what God had told her to do. I said God wanted Eve to bend her will to His will, and He is asking all of us to do the same thing.

As those words came out of my mouth, I remember thinking they were way too far above the kids' heads. I was about to say it another way when Connor's voice broke through. His question was clear. It was articulate. And it could've slipped from the mouth of any adult in big service.

"Keggie," he said. "What if I don't want to bend my will?"

Whoa. And there we were. The entire room seemed to wait for the answer. Kids, little people, all listening as if Connor's bold question had touched some deep place in every one of them. Because, of course, it had. Who can understand the way God's Spirit works in man's heart? Even little hearts.

Before it was over, Connor had made the most critical choice of his young life. He asked Jesus to live in His heart and help him obey God. Did we handle it with great care? You better believe it. Is Connor getting further age-appropriate instruction and prayer support? Absolutely. I love how Connor's daddy put it later. "It's the first step," Patrick said, "to a lifetime of following Jesus." Amen.

I understood what lay behind my sweet Connor's honest question. My me monster always thinks she'll be happier if she has her way. She lives convinced that appeasing her own wishes is the key to living her best life. She is woefully deceived and mightily persistent. *Please me*, says the me monster. *Make me look good*, she insists. *Defend me. Satisfy me. Make me happy at all costs, or else.* ("Or else" is never pretty.)

I'm grateful Connor bowed his heart to Jesus that day, but my grandson will continue to discover what all believers learn as they start out in a new life with Christ. Our me monsters aren't automatically silenced by our new birth. God doesn't perform spiritual lobotomies on us, strategically removing our inclination to favor self over surrender. Instead, He gives time and opportunity to learn the secret of living by dying, of discovering His Spirit within us to empower us, if we'll choose His will over our own.

You Can't Have a Resurrection Without a Crucifixion

We speak in the church of deciding to follow Christ. Jesus didn't use any such language. He talked about surrendering our lives to gain His.

Over and over, God allows us to meet with situations and people requiring us to die to what we want if we're going to yield to what He says. But spiritual death doesn't appeal to us any more than physical death. Living the resurrected life with Christ? We like the promise—but wish we could get there without dying. But we can't, regardless of how often we share Scripture memes on our social media accounts. If we're wondering why there's no power in our Christian walk, we might ask ourselves if we're hoping for a resurrection where there's been no crucifixion. That's the real tragedy of stiffening our wills instead of yielding them: If we don't die to ourselves, we'll never know the joy of Christ in us, and all the audacious promises of Scripture will be only words on a page.

We act as if our choices are casual, independent, and isolated. The reality is they cause us to forfeit the privilege of knowing the power and presence of Christ to work out through us what the Cross worked in us. We can't choose to disregard God's voice of correction and instruction and expect to hear Him encourage us, lead us, and comfort us. God isn't divisible.

Listen to the words of Jesus from John 14:19-21:

"After a little while, the world will no longer see Me; but you will see Me; because I live, you will live also. In that day you will know that I am in my Father, and you in me, and I in you.

"He who has My commandments and keeps them is the one who loves Me, and he who loves Me will be loved by My Father, and I will love Him and disclose Myself to him" (NASB).

To have Jesus make himself known to us, we must enthrone Him as the authority of our lives by yielding to His will and ignoring ours. We move forward by falling before Him, and we fill up by emptying ourselves out for His purposes.

Hear ye, hear ye. I can't imagine a better place to sound a crucial warning. This is where we can slip backwards. If we're not careful, we'll get all wiggy and try to gut out our obedience. Quit that! We don't want to try harder to do better, remember? We want to *lean* harder, and trust Jesus to strengthen our dusty frames from the inside out. We're learning to say yes and amen to Jesus's word, "Without me you can do nothing!" We're learning we can't manage our sins through the strength of our willpower and we're learning to rely on Jesus to make us victorious over them.

Trying harder is religion's trap. It's fueled by fear and guilt, and it will fail us every time, but deep (and wide!) satisfaction is the delightful surprise of grace-driven obedience. Hear the encouraging words of Paul in Galatians 5:16: *If we walk by the Spirit, we won't carry out the desires of the flesh.* (You can read "the desires of the flesh" as your "me monster.")

It's crucial for us to understand what Paul is saying and what he isn't saying. The apostle didn't tell us not to carry out the desires of the flesh and we would walk by the Spirit. That's the failed religion of legalism. He also didn't say that if we walk by the Spirit, we won't have to *contend with* the desires of our flesh. That's wishful thinking!

Paul said if we walk by the Spirit, we won't *carry out* the desires of the flesh. Why? Because when we walk with Christ, yielded to His Spirit in us, His victory over sin is ours! It all boils down to the power of one ongoing realization and constant confession: We need Jesus in the worst way, every day. We can't live for Him without living with Him. We can't choose the crucified life and live it apart from Him, but the Spirit of God is beyond faithful to teach us the surrendered way. He'll show us where the traps are, if we ask. And ask we must, because we never graduate to a place where we aren't susceptible to them. From Genesis to Revelation, we find the enemy trying to lure us into sin with variations of the same snare he laid in the garden. If you'll remember, Eve took of the fruit because it appealed to her appetite, her desire for beauty, and her desire for wisdom.

We see those same longings in the following warning from 1 John 2:15-17, and it smacks our twenty-first-century selves in the foreheads. *Do not love the world nor the things in the world. If anyone loves the world, the love of the Father is not in him. For all that is in the world, the lust of the flesh and the lust of the eyes and the boastful pride of life, is not from the Father, but is from the world. The world is passing away, and also its lusts; but the one who does the will of God lives forever* (NASB).

Satan tempts us with the lust of the flesh, the lust of the eyes, and the pride of life by all manner of disguise. And oh, is he subtle. He'll even tempt us to find our satisfaction and purpose in the pursuit of God rather than in God, in our knowledge of the Word rather than the Word, and in the approval of other believers rather than the favor of God.

To illustrate, we'll close this chapter out with a story. It doesn't paint me in the best light, but it's worth it if you see God's faithfulness in my ugly. You're about to get a sneak peek into my prayer journal. The setting is a hunting lodge in the woods of Mississippi where the women of my church were meeting for a ladies retreat. The rest will be embarrassingly self-explanatory …

Hello Jesus! You and I both know one of my most oft-repeated prayers for years now has been to die to me, that I might gain You.

"I have been crucified with Christ, and it is no more I who live, but Christ who lives in me. And the life I now live, I live by faith in the Son of God who gave Himself for me."

I know Paul said it first but it's my goal, too. I want to know the fullest possible realization of them.

I'm not there.

Surprised? No, of course You aren't. Sometimes I feel farther from those words being my reality than I do at others. I've said many times that self has a thousand lives and I've often tried to list all the ways self tries to thrive:

Self interest
Self-involvement
Self-protection

Self-reliance
Selfishness
Self defense
Self-improvement
Self-importance
Self-promotion
Self-awareness
Self-sufficient
Self-consciousness
Self-righteousness

Wow. And those are just a few! You've taught me that self will go to any lengths to survive—even engaging in "Christian" activities, if self gets to live and have its way, using its own resources. Self is proficient at forming a crust that must be habitually surrendered to God …

Jesus, it's like the more I long for You and the more I love You, the more of this monstrous self I see. Why, I even see self's effort to protect self in the way I hesitate to talk too much about this subject with other believers, even though self is like the boogey man in a bad movie that refuses to stay dead, coming back scene after scene, despite what looks like one death blow after another. Self is smart, in a human wisdom way, and self wants to live, so self likes to tell me if I keep talking about this people will decide I must be way more selfish than the average believer!

I guess that could be true, but I think something else is at work here. I suspect You are behind my awareness of this increasing and ongoing need to live crucifying self. You're answering my prayers to teach me how to lose me to know the fullest possible life in You. I don't think we begin to see our selfishness until we start asking you to search it out in us, and root it out of us.

Slow and steady You are at this. Gentleness marks You, and I'm so grateful. Without a doubt, I couldn't handle seeing all the ugly in me at once. I'm glad You're patient and faithful to finish what You've begun in me. Just not all at once. And that brings me to this weekend. Yesterday felt weird. And it caught me my surprise.

I didn't expect to feel out of place when we arrived, but I did. It was like I didn't know how to be in this type of gathering anymore without being one of the speakers. That feeling of not fitting in, it came unexpectedly because I was so looking forward to soaking it all up instead of bringing a message. Or, so, I thought …

Once the conference room where we would be having sessions was ready and I'd helped the girls that were leading the event set up as much as I could, though they really didn't need me, I found this quiet place for the two of us. I wanted to hear from You. I wanted to understand how I was feeling, and I've learned to love the way you speak. For me, Your voice often comes as a dawning, a layer-upon-layer realization. It starts as a glimmer of understanding and builds into undeniable brilliance. It reminds me of how the sun rises and the light increases by increments until its full strength is unmistakable.

Insight came that way yesterday, and it's growing. You're doing it, aren't You? You're answering more of my losing-self prayers this weekend! You're letting me lose more of me so I can encourage others You're calling forward. You're giving me an opportunity to be their prayer support. Wow. I see it now and I'm amazed all over again at how self shrinks back when self feels threatened.

I see yet again that I must trust Christ to die daily to all the "selves." I can't die to self without your help any more than I can stockpile grace, mercy, peace, etc. These blessings are mine *in Christ*, not in me. In me is no good thing, including the power to crucify self. I can only abide in Christ and there, in the abiding, I am and can be dead to self and alive to You.

As for the pain of decreasing that You might increase. I wonder … How do I expect self to be decreased, unless self is decreased?! I claim to understand I can't abide in You without living at the end of me, but I keep managing to forget death is painful, don't I?

So, yes, it did feel awkward, at first. I've figured out the right word for how I was feeling. Awkward. It felt awkward. But now? Now it feels good and right and divine and planned and purposed. You are closer to me than what I think is me and my will is all that ever lies between us. I am in you and you are in me and we are in the Father. Oh, to daily lay me down at the Blessed Door and live in the Heaven of Your will.

Stay at it, Holy Spirit. I know this isn't the last lesson in dying to self, not by any means, but I get this one, Lord. I do. Stay with me, Jesus. Keep showing me how to live dying. You are worthy, and life with You is worth it.

That's a wrap on the journal entry. Ironically, putting it out there in black and white has left me feeling vulnerable before you but clothed by the protective love of God. That's a solid good trade. I double-dog dare you to ask Jesus to help you die to yourself and live to Him. And then, keep asking, and watch Him become your delight.

Questions for Group Study or Private Reflection

1. What heart habit does Shellie recommend in the opening pages of this chapter? How do you feel about adopting it?
2. In your own words, what is a me monster, and do you think you have one?
3. Was there any part of the rather embarrassing excerpt of Shellie's prayer journal you could relate to, and why?

Chapter Sixteen

· · · · ·

All You Can Carry

*"We have all eternity to celebrate the victories
but only a few hours before sunset to win them."*

—AMY CARMICHAEL

I don't know if it goes against her Southern raising, or if it comes out of her own love of family, but my mama does not like to see anyone leave her house emptyhanded.

It's as predictable as sunrise following sunset. When I start to leave my parents' house, Mama, whom I affectionately call The Queen of Us All, sets out to load me up with whatever she can find on hand. There's a bit of banana pudding in the refrigerator? Good, she'll send it to my man. Do I need an outfit to wear to my next speaking event? I'm in the right place. Charlotte's Clothes Closet is open for business. (That's a good thing. I'm pretty much missing the female shopping gene, at least where it comes to clothes. But I'll wear you slap out in a bookstore.)

My sisters and I have all learned that to compliment Mama on anything in her house or on her body means she will try to give it to us at her earliest opportunity. And don't get me started on what she wants to give to whom once she slips out of this world. Mama's been making that list for years. Our part in all this gift-giving? Be willing to receive. Nothing pleases Mama like seeing us leave her presence with our hands full.

Can I tell you what I've learned? God likes giving to His kids, too! It's the basis of my third heart habit. For the last couple of chapters, I've been sharing with you some of the ways I've learned to enjoy God, even when my heart feels cold and indifferent. Let's recap.

I've recommended the vital practice of learning to approach God on the finished work of Christ Jesus instead of trying to relate to Him based on anything you have or haven't done. Quit trying to earn God's favor and start living in it. Quit trying harder to do better. Own your neediness. Run through the Door that is Christ Jesus empty-handed, admitting nothing you've done or could ever do has earned you this great inheritance, but you're gratefully determined to live in it!

I've also recommended a daily surrendering. Dying to live means taking your eyes off yourself, ignoring you, and placing them squarely on Jesus. Some of you might still be thinking, *But, Shellie, the Bible tells us to examine our hearts. What do you do with that?*

You're right, and indeed it does. *Test yourselves to see if you are in the faith; examine yourselves! Or do you not recognize this about yourselves, that Jesus Christ is in you—unless indeed you fail the test?* (2 Corinthians 13:5 NASB)

The problem we can encounter is our tendency to start with us, get mired down by us, and end in the same place, trying to figure out what's wrong with us. Truth is, we can't heal ourselves, but we can lose ourselves in the Healer—so quit trying to analyze the crevices of your own heart. I wrote a good bit about this in my book *Heart Wide Open,* but it's important, and considering the ongoing joy I'm discovering in ignoring me, I'm going to try to say it a different way.

Introspection is necessary and good, but it can also be a trap that's easy to fall into and hard to escape. We must learn to lay our hearts open and ask God to show us anything we need to confess, address any behaviors we need to change, and then move on, trusting Him with the cleansing. If we think we can weed our own hearts, we'll be prisoners of our own search parties, and they all meet the same dead end, eventually. Oh, and while we're here, the same rules apply to what we think we may have gotten right. Forgetaboutit! We find the deep and wide life in ignoring our successes and our failures to fixate on Jesus.

And now for our third biblical antidote to a passionless heart. Like the first two, it comes straight out of my personal experience, and it will sound ridiculously simple. That's because it *is* ridiculously simple.

I'm not immune to those times when I've yielded to God with my eyes fixed on Jesus and wrenched off me and my concerns only to discover—surprise!—God still seems nowhere to be found. When I find myself there, I trust my cold heart to Him and begin piling up prayers for others. I'll set out with the goal of loading my arms up through prayer with as many heavenly blessings as I can think of for as many people as I can think of, aiming to see them come to Jesus or draw closer if they already know Him.

I'll begin to pray for that one's salvation and this one's healing, for deliverance from addiction this one needs or a deeper hunger for the Word of God for a believer who seems lukewarm and settled. If I need prayer starters, I pull out my smart phone and refresh my memory with prayer requests I've recorded on my notepad app from people I've met along the way. I'll ask for healing of heart wounds and physical injuries. I'll ask for reconciliation between those who are at odds, and I'll pray for the restoration of marriages I know to be teetering on the brink.

I've left names out on purpose, but you get my point. Let's quit insulting God by wondering where He is and if He is listening when His Word declares He is always with us, never leaving us or forsaking us. Start there, on the nekkid faith of His Word. ("Nekkid" is a good

Southern word meaning "unclothed." Don't try to dress yourself in anything else.) If we're struggling in prayer, we can say something like, "Lord, I don't know what's wrong with me today, but I trust you to tell me anything I need to know." And then we can choose to trust we're in God's favor through Christ Jesus and remind ourselves He loves to give good gifts to His children.

We come with empty hands, acknowledging we can't come through the Door with yesterday's performance or tomorrow's intentions. We can't come through the Door with what we want to do or what we didn't do. We come nekkid, clothed in nothing but the righteousness of Christ, but we leave with grace for others. We leave with forgiveness for this person, mercy for that one. We can leave with our arms full of spiritual blessings to take to the world!

Let's learn to sit before God and let Him bring other people to our minds who need healing, deliverance, and hope. It's impossible to run out of things to pray about for other people! For Heaven's sake, we can't run out of prayer requests lifting the needs of our own families. Can I get a witness?

Joining God in His passion for all His children rebounds in the most surprising way. We can start with a cold heart, but we'll find it warming beneath His eternal flame. God is a win/win God. When we bring the sacrifice of self, He brings the fire.

So, that's number three. Ask, a lot. Put your worries into words. Ask for massive things and small things. Ask for yourself, yes, but ask more for others. Arrive empty-handed, acknowledging you have no credentials of your own but you're standing in matchless grace, and determine to leave with your arms full. When we ignore ourselves to pray for others, God will meet personal needs we've never even mentioned.

Heart Habit Number 3: Come empty-handed, leave with your arms full.

I realize I've given you a lot to remember over the last couple of chapters. I'm about to give you an acronym that helps me recall them. I sum up those three reminders with three letters: WIP

Worship God. That's the first heart habit we discussed, celebrating our access through Christ and relying on His Spirit.

Ignore yourself. That's the dying to self of our second heart habit.

Pray for others. That's the asking plan. Ask, ask, ask. Get grace, give grace. Get forgiven, forgive others. Soak in love so you can soak someone in love.

Many years ago, in a time known as the '80s, when shoulder pads and leg warmers were all the rage and feathered hair was everything, my friends and I danced to a song called "Whip It," by Devo. It carried some social controversy, but that sailed right over our big-haired heads. We weren't that deep. We just liked the beat, and the lyrics were catchy. Today, when my flesh tries to keep me out of God's Presence, I remember what He has taught me. "I *WIP* it and I whip it good." (You poor babies out there will need to google that song to get that but consider yourselves warned. The tune stays with a person.)

I wish I could see your face right now. I don't know if you're frowning or laughing or torn between the two, but as I've been known to tell my audiences, "I take God seriously. Myself, not so much!" I know me. I wake up with me and I go to bed with me and I can't get away from myself at any time in between. My stories might not be typical, and my word associations may strike you as odd, but the habits I propose are all grounded in Scripture, and they're opening up a sweeter, closer, more fulfilling life with God than I ever dreamed I could live, even though the Word promised such living and Jesus secured it.

Our enemy would have us believe a life where Jesus is our one great obsession must be dry and boring, that we must live ever so carefully so as not to fall, balanced precariously on whatever tiny piece of ground we've managed to secure. I have a word for that. Baloney! (That's Southern Louisiana Greek for any intellectual readers.)

To live with our eyes fixed on Jesus, seeking to know the fullness of all that is ours through Him, is to live in a broad place! It's a satisfying space where there's plenty room to live and breathe. *For this reason I bow my knees before the Father, from whom every family in heaven and on earth derives its name, that He would grant you, according to the riches of His glory, to be strengthened with power through His Spirit in the inner man, so that Christ may dwell in your hearts through faith; and that you, being rooted and grounded in love, may be able to comprehend with all the [saints what is the breadth and length and height and depth, and to know the love of Christ which surpasses knowledge, that you may be filled up to all the fullness of God* (Ephesians 3:14-19 NASB).

Helping others live in this deep, wide love of Jesus is why I've done my best in these pages to let you see a real woman in love with Jesus. Holding up an edited version who seems so far ahead of where most of us live helps no one, and I refuse to risk anyone losing hope in the face of pretend perfection.

The truth is, while I've been stone-cold honest in what I've said, I haven't told you the half of my ugly. I've told you how hard my heart once was and how I wanted Jesus to secure me an eternal home, if He would just leave me be to do my own thing until I hit the streets of gold. But I've had other things in my heart, seriously sacrilegious things God saw and heard before the thoughts finished forming.

I live in wonder that not only did He refrain from striking me silly, He taught me to delight in Him and His Word, called me into women's ministry, and granted me the privilege of serving Him.

That same woman. That's grace. Grace upon grace.

It makes me want to tell everyone who will listen that Jesus is the healer of all things broken and we can't work up affection for Him. So quit! Dare instead to seek His face and let Him breathe new life into your heart.

I'm convinced the things I've shared with you in these pages will help anyone who longs for more of Jesus than they're experiencing and who is willing to own his or her need. But then, that brings us to a litmus test that will divide us into two camps: dry unfulfilled settlers, or increasingly passionate seekers.

Do You Have Enough Jesus?

If you're okay with your experience of Christ, I don't suppose anything I've said will be of use to you. And that would be tragic. I'll ask you again.

Do you have enough Jesus?

Are you okay with knowing *of* Jesus but not knowing how to nourish yourself in His Presence? You are the only one who can answer that question.

Sit with it while we look at Mark 8:22-25. This passage can crystallize the choice for us. We'll begin reading as a blind man is brought to Jesus for healing.

And they came to Bethsaida. And they brought a blind man to Jesus and implored Him to touch him. Taking the blind man by the hand, He brought him out of the village; and after spitting on his eyes and laying His hands on him, He asked him, "Do you see anything?"

And he looked up and said, "I see men, for I see them like trees, walking around."

Then again He laid His hands on his eyes; and he looked intently and was restored, and began to see everything clearly (NASB).

This is a fascinating story. As far as I can tell, this is the sole time in the Bible where we not only see Jesus heal someone in stages, but we get to watch Him pray, stop, and basically ask the person, "Is it working?"

Wow. Here's what we know. We can trust the One who made the man's eyes and who had already healed blind eyes had not hit a tough spot in his ministry. Jesus wasn't suddenly stymied and wondering why this wasn't working when he was doing it the same way he had done it before. In fact, Scripture would suggest that He never healed anyone the same way twice! So what is happening?

I wouldn't presume to tell you I know why the Bible records this story. I don't know why Jesus stopped and asked the man if he could see. I must believe He knew the answer before He asked the question. I will, however, tell you what I do know.

This man who once was blind but could now partially see could've decided the improvement in his sight after Jesus prayed the first time was enough for him. Having been totally blind before, this man could've settled for his new eyesight, even if it was fuzzy. He could've felt uncomfortable standing there with the friends who had brought him to Jesus while they waited.

Tick-tock, tick-tock.

He could've felt the pressure of the spotlight and knowing everyone was waiting to go to Cracker Barrel for lunch. And even though he couldn't see clearly just yet, he could've answered, "Yes, Jesus … I see," and then added "enough" under his breath when no one was listening.

And had the blind man done that, what he was seeing when Jesus stopped and asked if he could see might very well have been all he would ever see. We'll never know.

Again, I'm not saying this is why the incident is preserved for all time. I will say, without hesitation, whatever we're settling for in our relationship with Jesus is what we'll have.

I can't help but wonder how many believers spend our entire Christian lives right here in this moment with this partially blind man. I suspect it's a sizeable percentage. We've met Jesus and our spiritual eyes are sort of, kind of, opened. We know there must be more to this life in Christ because what we're experiencing in our believing lives doesn't compare to what the Bible advertises, but we decide to settle for what we know.

I mean, it's not like we're still blind. We see more than we once did. We're saved, after all, and headed to Heaven. There was a time when we couldn't see at all, and now we see, some, and so we decide that yes, what we are seeing is enough to see.

There's another way, another choice.

If we're not experiencing the fullness of all Jesus longs to give us, we can take the holy dare and quit pretending what we have is enough.

The first step in knowing more of this sweet Jesus is admitting we don't have enough and that we want more. I don't mind confessing this at all. I say it all the time.

I ran across an old hymn a few days ago, written in the 1800s. The prose was lengthy and full of "thees and thous," so with due respect and acknowledgement to one Mr. Theodore Monod, I've taken his ideas from the last lines of all four verses and whittled them into something I can hold onto and share. What follows describes the secret desires of my shameful heart when Jesus first began calling me to Himself, and it speaks to where He has brought me. It's an open-ended story because He is still writing it.

All of me, none of You,
Some of me, some of You,
Less of me, more of You,
None of me, all of You.

If I were going to plot out a timeline for those periods, "Some of me and some of You" would be the longest season of the four, by about three to one. But it didn't have to be. I'm praying my words will help someone, or a bunch of someones, pass through that leg of the journey far more quickly than I did.

I'll say it until I see Him face-to-face: "My name is Shellie, and I need more Jesus. I want more Jesus. I'm determined to spend my life running for the Door that is sweet Jesus."

If you're in, join me in the next chapter. I'll be talking about how we can train our eyes on Him and be transformed, not by our efforts, but by His Presence.

I am running for the Door.
See me running for the Door.
I am running for my life.
Run with me!

Questions for Group Study or Private Reflection

1. Can you identify a specific situation, isolated or ongoing, where you search your heart, ask for and receive forgiveness, and still feel mired in guilt and introspection? Write about it here.

2. Shellie's third recommended heart habit is about praying for others, coming to Jesus with your empty hands and leaving with your arms full. Find a Scripture that encourages such prayer.

3. Take Shellie's short verse and circle where you are right now. When you get back to this page, compose a written prayer about where you are and where you want to be.

Chapter Seventeen

· · · · ·

Beholding Glory

*"Beware of harking back to what you once were
when God wants you to be something you have never been."*

—OSWALD CHAMBERS

When I was a little girl, my Papa used to sing an old Jim Ed Brown tune. The twisting lines tickled me then and amuse me now.

*I was looking back to see
If you were looking back to see
If I was looking back to see
If you were looking back at me.
You were cute as you could be
Standing looking back at me
And it was plain to see
That I'd enjoy your company.*

The lyrics were written from a man to his sweetie, but they remind me of the God who created us for His pleasure, and knows our best life is finding Him as our greatest treasure, looking down to see if we're looking back at Him.

Through Jesus, God came looking for us because He wanted us. He is still taken with us, and He asks us to become taken with Him.

For the eyes of the LORD move to and fro throughout the earth that He may strongly support those whose heart is completely His (2 Chronicles 16:9 NASB).

God's eyes are forever roaming the earth looking for those who are completely His. It's when "our eyes meet" as the romance novels say, that the match strikes. To live looking at Him—not just once to escape death, but repeatedly—is to experience life, deep and wide.

God's asking us to spend our lives making eye contact with Him, and the marvel of His plan is the way this fixation transforms us and molds us into who He created us to be. We aren't changed by our good intentions or our best efforts, and Christ isn't formed in those who try harder to do better. We're transformed by this ongoing looking, or what the Bible calls beholding. His Presence transforms our broken "want-to"s.

You may wonder why I insist on using such an ancient word when you'll never hear me saying, "Behold, the new shirt I bought on sale!" Why not use a more familiar word? Because Scripture uses the word *beholding*, and it seems to carry more weight than familiar words like "seeing" or "looking."

To behold is to fix the eyes upon; to see with attention; to observe with care. *Behold, the Lamb of God who takes away the sin of the world!* (John 1:29 NASB)

To behold is to look or to direct the eyes to an object.

And I beheld, and lo, in the midst of the throne and of the four beasts, and in the midst of the elders, stood a Lamb, as it had been slain (Revelation 5:6 KJV).

To behold is to fix the attention upon an object; to attend; to direct or fix the mind. *Behold, I stand at the door and knock* (Revelation 3:20 NASB).

We could say the biblical word for beholding is more like, "Don't miss this!"; "Watch this!"; "Get this!"; or "Check this out." God is asking us to behold Him in order to see things His way, to see what we're seeing in a different way than we were seeing it before we came into relationship with Him; through beholding, He begins to open our eyes. Beholding God helps us see those we're in relationship with the way God sees them. Consider the scene that took place at the Cross.

When Jesus then saw His mother, and the disciple whom He loved standing nearby, He said to His mother, "Woman, behold, your son!" Then He said to the disciple, "Behold, your mother!" From that hour the disciple took her into his own household (John 19:26-27 NASB).

We know Mary and John could already see each other with their physical eyes. Jesus was asking his mother and his best friend to behold each other in a new light. This is the beholding we see in 2 Corinthians 3:18. Intentional looking is the secret of spiritual transformation.

But we all, with unveiled face, beholding as in a mirror the glory of the Lord, are being transformed into the same image from glory to glory, just as from the Lord, the Spirit (NASB).

Hear God saying, "Meet my eyes. See the way I see. Let your conclusions be formed by the Truth I reveal to you. See people and circumstance through my eyes. Meet my gaze. See life as I see it, and be transformed."

Way back in Chapter Four, we looked at the Fall of man and how it followed Eve training her gaze on—beholding, if you will—the tree God had deemed off limits and making up her own mind about it. Let's go back to the garden one final time.

Using what she might describe as rational thinking, Eve looked at something God said wasn't good and decided it was the very thing she needed to be healthy, wealthy, and wise, and that obeying God was keeping her from her best life. Eve was changed by what she beheld and what she concluded about what she beheld.

So are we.

This is the twisted thinking we inherited from the Fall: our susceptibility to the loud, incessant lie that we can find what we most need in the world around us. Truth? We don't know what the good life is, and we can't find it on our own.

Man was placed in the garden of God's fellowship with human faculties dialed in to God's Presence. He was able to touch, see, taste, hear, and feel all the tangible gifts and delights surrounding him. He was not free to enjoy it all, and he was encouraged to experience it all—if he agreed with what God said was good.

God knows what surrounds us on this planet can never satisfy our deepest desires. He continually calls us to look to Him for our best life. But if we draw other conclusions and fill our hearts, God's temple, with people and things, with whatever (or whomever) we deem necessary to make life worth living, we forfeit walking with Him in our heart, His garden.

The infinite Christ in us is God's answer for our cavernous desires, and our hearts begin to discover the best life when we begin to learn He is more than enough. He is the adventure of our lives, changing us from the inside out by His Supernatural Presence.

The biblical word for this ongoing process of becoming who we are in Christ Jesus is sanctification. It's what God has made available through Jesus and He means for us to become like Christ!

When we intentionally train our eyes on Christ, these dull senses of ours that have a renewed capacity to experience God because Christ dwells in us begin to recognize His Presence, and our spiritual eyes and ears continue to sharpen, from glory to glory. Or not.

We can come to faith and spend the rest of our lives seeing some and hearing a little because we're going it alone in our safety zones. The blessing of a life transformed by Christ is never forced on settlers. It's reserved for seekers.

"You will seek Me and find Me, when you seek Me with all of your heart" (Jeremiah 29:13 NASB).

We are pilgrims, designed for more. In Him, we can be satisfied without being settled, loved without being lazy, rest while ever reaching. If we get saved to sit down, we miss the delightful God-designed tension of living in pursuit of an inexhaustible and eternal Savior who satisfies us while creating a hunger for the only more that is forevermore.

Jesus, the Pilgrim's Hope

Jesus said the greatest commandment was to love God with our whole heart, soul, and strength. And we can, with His help! We don't become God-lovers at our salvation, and we don't become God-lovers by association with other believers or through the process of time. At conversion, we who were dead and couldn't love God have now become capable of loving Him.

Jesus knows we'll need Him in order to love Him. And if we'll live dying to our little "i" and keep our eyes on Him, we'll see it happen. It's our birthright! Press on until you can own the words of Peter.

And though you have not seen Him, you love Him, and though you do not see Him now, but believe in Him, you greatly rejoice with joy inexpressible and full of glory (1 Peter 1:8 NASB).

Isn't it crazy that Eve's simple act of continuing to behold the forbidden fruit led her to reach for what was evil and decide it was good, culminating in the Fall of Man? Yes, but consider the much more glorious plan of God! His plan for spiritual growth is ridiculously simple: fix your eyes on Jesus. The promise of Christ says I can truly come to prefer what He prefers, approve what He approves, and value what He values, all by beholding Him with a determined focus. A life of beholding the One who is truly good and reaching for Him reverses and redeems the effects of the Fall and restores the fellowship between God and man that was lost in the garden.

It begs a question we all need to answer: Are we beholding Jesus in the intentional way of 2 Corinthians 3:18? According to that verse, it's easy enough to know whether we are beholding Jesus, or not. If we're beholding Jesus, we'll be in the process of transformation. Put another way, you could say if we aren't changing, it's because we're not beholding. So which one describes us? Remember, we're looking at our own lives, not our neighbors'. I've prepared a few statements that may help or hurt. Just don't holler out loud if you don't want to give yourself away. Ready? Here we go.

If our testimony is always what God did and never what He is doing, we might be churching, but we aren't changing.

If we can tell you what we've learned but not what we're learning, we could be churching, but we aren't changing.

If we're content being served God's Word without feeding ourselves, we may be churching, but we won't be changing.

If we're grateful for grace and God's forgiveness but we refuse to offer grace and forgiveness to others, we may be churching, but we aren't changing.

If we rely on the grace of Christ to cover our sins but we don't rely on the power of His grace to quit sinning, we might be churching, but we aren't changing.

If we consider Sunday to be God's day and the other six to be ours, we might be churching, but we aren't changing.

If the only time we worship is when we're gathered with other believers, we may be churching, but we aren't changing.

If we're always asking for prayer but rarely praying, we might be churching, but we aren't changing.

I could go on, but each of us knows if we're churching or changing. (And even if we *are* changing, we can rest assured that we haven't arrived. Praise Him.) The blessed good news for each of us? Where we are doesn't have to be where we settle! You know the saying: nothing changes unless something changes. If we're breathing in and breathing out, we can learn to behold Jesus and become witnesses of God's provision—not only to bring us to Heaven, but to transform us on earth. Make no mistake, we'll bear the marks of where we linger longest, be it companionship with Christ, the world, or in the circular thinking of our own thoughts.

But, how, Shellie? How does transformation come from beholding? I'm going to answer that, but first, I need to remind you of something.

We're going to talk about obedience, but I don't want you to tune me out because this will not be a discussion of do's and don'ts.

I've been there, and I'm not going back. I'm a living example of someone who once trusted Jesus to save her but trusted her own efforts to walk that salvation out. As if the One who died for me that I might live in Him took off afterward with a cheery, "Do your best, and I'll see you on the other side!" That's hogwash. Pure hogwash.

In those days, I lived like it was all up to me to resist the enemy. I acted like the Holy Spirit was cheering me on from the sidelines when I prayed for help, not realizing He was with me to win the day if I would rely on His indwelling power instead of my willpower. Oh no, back then I would resolve to do better, fail miserably, and resolve again. I couldn't see that I was as powerless to work out my daily salvation in my own strength as I had been to save my eternal soul.

Sadly, I knew I couldn't get to Heaven on my efforts, but I was blind to the fact that my strivings weren't sanctifying me, either! And as long as I thought they were, I was frustrating the grace of Christ Jesus in pursuit of my own righteousness. Have mercy, here's what the Word says about that plan! *For if righteousness comes through the Law, then Christ died needlessly* (Galatians 2:21 NASB).

Ugh.

There's no comparison between that life and the one where we trust Jesus to deliver us from the power of sin the same way He delivered us from its guilt! It's why I ask Him to boss me. We're free from striving when He is governing. And far from living a narrow life of do's and don'ts, dying to live leaves us standing in the deep and wide expanse of His love.

Out of my distress I called on the LORD; *the* LORD *answered me and set me in a broad place* (Psalm 118:5 NRSV).

So, no, I'm not going back to legalism, and I don't want you to, either! But this isn't that. Man doesn't power this obedience. It's all new house rules. Let's have a quick recap.

In the Garden, God set down house rules Adam and Eve were supposed to follow to continue to enjoy His Presence. True? And then, there in the wilderness when God called Moses up to the mountain, He set forth house rules for those who wanted to know Him. True? All true.

And then came Jesus.

In Christ, in the glorious New Covenant, we're again given "rules of fellowship"—but this time it's as different as day and night, black and white, wrong and right! Unlike anything before it, this obedience is powered and empowered by God Himself. The self-effort of law keeping? Over! The "don't do this, but do that" of will-worship? Gone!

This is Christ, fully God and fully man, living in us and through us as we intentionally behold Him, empowering us to obey that we might abide. Heads up—good men and women don't win this fight, but spiritual paupers thrive!

Remember when Jesus taught *Blessed are the poor in spirit, for theirs is the kingdom of heaven* (Matthew 5:3 NASB)?

I believe this is some of what He was saying. Blessed is the one who understands all the blessings of Christ Jesus are *in Him*.

Blessed be the God and Father of our Lord Jesus Christ, who has blessed us with every spiritual blessing in the heavenly places in Christ (Ephesians 1:3 NASB).

This entire first chapter of Ephesians continues to stress this theme. Our strength, our hope, our empowerment is not in us but in Christ. We don't stockpile habits of grace like patience, wisdom, and mercy. We draw them from Christ as we need them, and oh, how we need them. Jesus is saying, "Blessed is the one who realizes this, who knows she has no strength to fight sin on her own, who stays close to Me to draw from Me. When she realizes she isn't up to the battle on her own, I am present as her Victory."

Blessed are we who realize we're perennially choice-challenged apart from Christ, owning the truth. We're in constant need of fresh eyes to see what He is seeing and fresh ears to hear what He is saying. Otherwise, we'll trust our own lying eyes and itchy ears by default. As we live beholding Jesus, we learn to see as He sees and do as He does, our lives confessing our belief that whatever action, thought, response, or habit He is requiring of us is what's best for us.

The more we live and abide with a determined focus on Jesus, the more we value His precepts, standards, commandments, etc., the more we *want* to do life His way.

In 1 John 5:2, John says, *"By this we know that we have come to know Him, if we keep His commandments"* (ESV). We could say it this way: When we see what God calls good and we call it good, too, we know we have come to love Him. This isn't knuckling down to try to change ourselves! This is beholding the One who is the same yesterday, today, and forever, and letting Him transform us from the inside out. This is how we'll experience the full offer of walking through life with God—by beholding Jesus. Remember when I said beholding Jesus reverses the Fall in our lives? We can make choices all day, every day that will result in Jesus transforming our lives.

And all we have to do is start now. I'll dive deeper into a story that illustrates everything I've been talking about here in the next chapter.

Questions for Group Study or Private Reflection

1. In your own words, explain what it would mean to go about your day beholding Jesus.
2. On the 0-10 scale, are you churching or changing?
3. What is the big difference between the obedience God asks of us and the "rules of fellowship" given to believers before the Cross?

Chapter Eighteen

· · · · ·

I Am Eve

*"If you can't see the sun you will be impressed with a street light.
If you've never felt thunder and lightning,
you'll be impressed with fireworks.
And if you turn your back on the greatness and majesty of God
you'll fall in love with a world of shadows and short-lived pleasures."*

—JOHN PIPER

A young woman named Jennifer messaged me last night and invited me to lunch. I could've asked for a rain check—because, you know, deadlines—but I found myself responding to her message almost before I knew it. I wanted her to feel loved and valued, and I knew putting our lunch date off wouldn't send that message.

See, over the last few years, three sweet young women have asked me to mentor them. My response each time, "Yes, of course!" Unfortunately, I had more enthusiasm than understanding of what that would look like (a recurring theme in my life), and at least one of the proposed mentees lived states away, so my mentoring game has been hit and miss. I do a lot of life with the other two young women, but saying I've mentored them would be a stretch. Which brings me back to Jennifer, the fourth young woman to ask me to mentor her. I may be slow, but I can recognize a pattern, eventually.

The night she asked me to mentor her, I jumped on it so quickly I may have scared her! I told her the woeful history of my mentoring efforts, and I admitted I didn't know what mentoring looked like or how to do it, but I was game. Jennifer said she didn't know what it meant either. We agreed to figure it out together, and that's why I was having lunch with a young wife and mother my daughter's age.

Our conversation was all pleasant chit-chat—until the moment it took a God-orchestrated turn. Even now I'm not quite sure how we went from small talk to Jennifer saying she could see my desire for the things of God and she wished she was more like that. I told her I had not always wanted more Jesus. We talked a bit about my story with Him, how the turning point for me began when I learned to admit what He already knew: that I didn't love Him or His Word the way I should, but I wanted to! I asked Jennifer if she had learned to pray that way.

She paused and gave me a general answer. Shortly afterward, the floodgates opened.

"The thing is," Jennifer began, "I have an eating problem and a spending problem. And that's just for starters. Mostly, I just have a problem wanting more of everything, and the same thing keeps happening. I know I'm going to end up regretting buying something I thought I just had to have or eating too much of the wrong things, and then I do it anyway! And then I regret it, like I knew I would. But I still keep doing it!"

I told Jennifer our hearts, hers and mine, are cavernous. Whatever we have, we want more of. I told her it has the potential to be a wonderful thing. We always want more because God put eternity in us and we're meant to keep reaching for Him, exploring

His Word and living the adventure of Him, but instead, we keep reaching for more of what we can grasp around us.

"Like Eve," I said. And I began to tell Jennifer how I was in the middle of writing a book about the life we settle for as opposed to the life we're meant to live. I was telling her about the conclusions Eve made that led to the Fall and how they mirror ours today when Jennifer's clear blue eyes met mine.

"I am Eve," she said, with startling clarity.

My heart caught.

"We are all Eve," I told her. "The sin we're infected with is thinking God isn't enough and what's available in this world is more promising. We want us and what we want more than we want God and what He wants. Not addressing this evil bottom line of not preferring God will always leave us fighting the wrong battle, trying to do what's right to please Him rather than being so pleased *by* Him that we do what's right. But God can teach us how to choose well, if we'll ask and keep asking." (By this time, I had begun to wish we were recording our exchange, so that's by no means verbatim, but it's close.)

Jennifer nodded vigorously, and her conversation shifted. "And then there's my marriage. We're about to celebrate our tenth anniversary and nothing is wrong. Everything is right! His new job, our house, our kids, everything! But it's like something is missing."

I told Jennifer I believe God graciously unsettles us when we get comfortable with where we are so we'll reach for Him. It's a holy dissatisfaction meant to get us up and moving toward Him. The danger comes when we try to fix it when we fill it with everything and everyone except the One we really need.

I saw another light-bulb moment flash in Jennifer's eyes! "Wow. That's us! That's me. Ethan and I were happiest when we were praying together over things, like our house and his job. We were always talking about God's will and things like that. But then, well, we got the house and the job, and we sort of stopped, like we didn't know what to pray for anymore." As Jennifer connected the dots between that and the earlier part of our conversation about over-indulgence, our conversation circled back to the power of asking Holy Spirit to help us choose well, to choose Jesus and keep choosing Him.

This, friends, is the opportunity for all of us, to write a vastly different open-ended script than the one from the Garden.

Eve studied the forbidden fruit and decided it was "good for food." Jesus says, *"I am the Bread of Life."* (John 6:48 NASB)

You and I have our own choice to make today and tomorrow. We can look for things and people in this world to satisfy our cavernous hearts, or we can choose to say, "Jesus, you are the bread that satisfies." We can tell Him we choose the Living Bread, and we can ask Him to teach us to hunger for more.

Eve concluded the tree was "lovely to behold," and in Song of Solomon 5:16, we read, *His mouth is most sweet, yes, he is altogether lovely. This is my beloved, and this is my friend, O daughters of Jerusalem!* We get this same choice. We can agree Jesus is a sight for these sore earthly eyes of ours that are bombarded with what the world says is lovely to behold and necessary for fulfillment. And we can say, "Jesus, you are beautiful to behold. Help me see Your beauty and value You more every day."

Eve decided the forbidden tree held wisdom she needed to reach out and grasp. According to Colossians 2:2-3, the sum of all wisdom and knowledge is in Christ Jesus: *That their hearts may be encouraged, having been knit together in love, and attaining to all the wealth that comes from the full assurance of understanding, resulting in a true knowledge of God's mystery, that is Christ Himself, in whom are hidden all the treasures of wisdom and knowledge.* We get to redeem the Fall by choosing to say, "Jesus, You are my standard, my authority, today and every day." We can declare truth over our lives. Christ is wisdom. We can choose the Word of God as our authority and ask Jesus to help us yield to Him.

You and I are susceptible to fallen moments that mimic Eve's, but Jesus, the Living Word of God, invites us to an all-you-can-eat buffet. And, praise Him, the more we feed on Him, the more of Him we will crave, until we discover, to our astonished delight, that He is transforming our desires, redeeming those fallen moments, and our hearts are proclaiming, "Jesus, you truly are good for food, a delight to behold, and desirable to make me wise. I take from you and I eat, and I give to others that they may eat."

These aren't simply choices we can make to teach us how to live a good, full, life. They are life-and-death choices we can be tragically slow to see.

Recently, I watched a very dear friend lose a battle with alcohol addiction. I often think about him. I tried so hard to help. I think of all the things I said to him—and those I didn't say. I've never been addicted to drugs or alcohol, but I can testify to the only hope we have of being set free and living free of our cavernous hearts.

If we don't determine Jesus alone is the Bread of Life and learn to nourish ourselves with Him, we will live reaching for our hit of choice—because a will that isn't submitted leads to a life that isn't satisfied. And whatever our fix, it will demand increasingly more of us until we discover what all addicts know: Addiction is hell.

And I'm talking to all of us now, for we are all addicts; it's only what we "use" that differs.

Beyond the addictions of drugs and alcohol trails a mile-long list of life-stealing traps. Food, pornography, shopping, sex, computer games, social media, gambling, work, exercise, and the one I fought for so long—my right to myself. I wanted the security of an eternity with God later while protecting and enjoying my right to myself in the here and now.

I'm convinced I stand on strong biblical ground when I say this addiction confronts us all. Holding onto "little i" is what keeps us from knowing the Great I Am. The boss of "little i" leaves us mired in the cage of inertia without realizing we're holding the key.

Life at the End of Me Street

Not long ago, I met a woman slightly older than me at a retreat where I was speaking. She laughed at my jokes (even the cheesy ones), took careful notes during my messages, and visited with me between the sessions. She'd already endeared herself to me when she leaned in close to whisper something in my ear as I was about to leave. "Pray for me," she said. "I've been in church all my life, but I've never been able to feel assured of my salvation. I ask Jesus to save me all the time, again and again. I don't know what's wrong with me."

All I could offer her was my experience. I told her when our goal is to settle the issue of our salvation rather than knowing and enjoying Jesus, we leave ourselves open for the enemy to assault us. We create the space he fills with doubts. He'll keep suggesting we aren't saved and, outside of the assurance we could have if we lived to know Him, we're defenseless. We'll live forever in this limbo. That's so not biblical.

We can't live as addicts to everything around us, trying to satisfy ourselves, and know the width, depth, length, and height of what Jesus has done for us. It's always either/or. What we think of as "ourselves" is nothing more than a hodgepodge of our past experiences, influences, and environment. What God wants is for us to find ourselves in Him and experience the joy of living convinced that "He is mine and I am His."

A dear friend who has walked the hellish journey of drug addiction and now lives in victory on the other side once told me it wasn't just the fear of giving up today's pill that held her captive for so long as she was taking a two-steps-forward-and-one-step-back trek out of her addiction. It was giving up the choice of returning to her drug down the road … if life got too hard.

This addict right here gets that, too.

I know how it feels to try to give up something to Jesus today while retaining the right to handle it my way tomorrow. Zero victory there. The lure of independent autonomy is a strong one, but we can't abide in Christ while nurturing our right to us, either in the present or the future. Like every other addict, we're presented each day with another opportunity to choose well.

While dying to ourselves to live in Christ is painful, I've found jumping on my grave is also delicious freedom! I choose to jump and jump again because I delight to find Jesus at the end of me! No, self isn't fond of death, but the true adventure of life in Christ begins where we end.

Questions for Group Study or Private Reflection

1. How did you feel when Jennifer said, "I am Eve"?
2. Can you relate to how dissatisfaction can be a blessed tool God uses to draw us into deeper relationship with Him but can also be dangerous? Why?
3. How does the enemy use our willingness to settle for eternal security over knowing and enjoying Jesus? Would you say your faith experience supports this? Why or why not?

Chapter Nineteen

. . . . .

How to Know What You Don't Know

*"The Christian is a holy rebel loose in the world
with access to the throne of God."*

—A. W. TOZER

Would it be safe? Should I, or shouldn't I?

I stood holding the open door of my vehicle, weighing a decision. I was staying at a small condo on the beach where I'd retreated to work on the words you're reading. I was headed to a nearby restaurant for dinner, laptop in tow, in case incredible inspiration struck while I was waiting for my meal. And of course, I had my purse with me. But now the beach was calling. It'd be too late for my evening walk if I waited until after dinner. *Go now, or don't go? Would it be safe? Should I, or shouldn't I?*

As I was contemplating my next move, I noticed a white van on the other side of my Suburban. A large man was sitting in the driver's seat with the door open, and he seemed to be watching me. When I caught his gaze, he looked away. This happened several times. As it was playing out, an old truck with three men, slumped down in some serious low-riding, rolled to a stop behind me. Great. I was blocked in, unless I asked them to move. I was growing more uncomfortable by the second when the guys in the truck began talking to the one in the van in a language I couldn't understand. Even better.

What should I do? I wanted to walk on the beach, but dare I lock my laptop and purse in the car and take my keys with these strangers witnessing my every move? Would I come back to a smashed-in window and stolen belongings? Was my drama bone making all of this up, or should I run for the safety of my second-floor apartment ASAP?

I prayed. And waited. When peace came, I made my decision: I locked up my valuables and headed for the beach.

Did I mention it was March, and the most unseasonably cold March in recent years at that? Right. Jesus and I pretty much had the beach to ourselves. I walked, we talked, and it was good. Just what I needed. And my Suburban? I returned to everything just as I'd left it. I went to dinner feeling silly about my earlier fears.

By the evening of the next long writing day I was mentally exhausted and ready for another stroll. It was even colder, so I bundled up in a sweatshirt and headed out for a prayer walk. Like the day before, the beach was empty, until I started back. As I began to near my condo, something in the ocean caught my eye. I squinted. *Wait?! That's not a something, that's a* someone!

No one had been swimming in the frigid ocean that week. No one. But this guy—at least it looked like a male—wasn't just swimming. He was celebrating! Clad only in a pair of shorts, the cavorting human reminded me of a dolphin as he jumped, dove, and waved. I pulled my eyes from him to see who he was waving at and saw a second man, a large man, standing on the beach holding a shirt. Our jubilant swimmer's shirt, no doubt. This was crazy! And they were positioned opposite the boardwalk I needed to take to get to my condo. I was about to meet some new friends.

As I drew near enough to speak above the wind, the large man looked my way and smiled. Surprise! It was the man from the white van! I returned his smile, motioned to his friend who was still playing in the chest-deep water, and said something about the temperature. His gestures told me he didn't understand. I pointed to my head and made the universal sign for "crazy," adding a broad smile to make sure I wasn't offensive. The large man returned my grin and nodded in agreement.

Our communication efforts exhausted, I turned to go in, but the whole scene was so strange I began to wonder if there was something more here, something I needed to understand. I stopped to sit on one of the lounge chairs that was still out, whispered a few more words of prayer, and waited.

Moments later, the swimmer made his way back to the beach. He took his shirt from the other man and used it as a towel. They exchanged words I couldn't understand, and the larger man headed back toward the condos. The swimmer headed in my direction. Clearly, he was coming to talk. I barely had time to wonder if we'd be able to communicate before he drew near enough to greet me in broken English, and we began to chat. We had to repeat ourselves and use a few hand motions, but we did a fair job of understanding each other. I found out it was my new friend's first time to see the ocean, let alone swim in it. He told me he was praising God for the water and the salt and the setting sun.

"Ah," I said, "So you're a believer."

The young man's face couldn't have exploded into a larger smile without breaking. "Oh, yes," he said. "Jesus is everything!"

And just like that we were siblings—gender, age, and culture notwithstanding, both in love with Jesus. As we jabbered about His goodness, I stuck out my hand. "I'm Shellie."

"I'm David," my new friend said. He motioned in the direction the larger guy took, and added, "That was my brother, Jonathan. He's not rude. He just can't speak English that well. Our other brother Abraham is with us. They're probably waiting for me at the truck."

David? Of course your name is David, and Jonathan was holding your shirt while you danced before the Lord. Of course. David, Jonathan, and Abraham. Three of the four men I had imagined beating and robbing me the day before. No one's ever going to believe this.

I learned David and his siblings were in construction. The night before they'd been driving around trying to find a condo that was scheduled for repairs. David also told me his mother gave them all biblical names because she wanted them to follow Jesus. With utmost sincerity, he said, "Jonathan is really—how do you say it, Shellie?— 'on fire' for Jesus, and he teaches me so much Bible."

Of course he does.

We had a few more minutes of conversation before David mentioned his waiting brothers again. I asked if we could pray together before he left and he agreed, excitedly. But then I sensed David stayed excited often. Afterward, I sat alone, smitten by God all over again. *What was this?* I asked.

Call to Me and I will answer you, and I will tell you great and mighty things, which you do not know (Jeremiah 33:3 NASB).

I didn't hear a voice in my head, but a gentle question materialized in my heart with familiar weight. *I wonder how many other things you think you know that you don't?*

Are you kidding? I wanted to holler to the skies! Many things! Countless things! Clearly, I know nothing! "Teach me things I don't know," I said to this Jesus who dwells in my heart. And I laughed right out loud as I added, "You can pretty much start anywhere!"

This is life spent deep and wide, listening for the God who still speaks, and it's not reserved for a chosen few. God speaks to those who make hearing from Him a priority, and we learn to recognize His Voice by listening to His Word. *Blessed is the man who listens to me, watching daily at my gates, waiting at my doorposts* (Proverbs 8:34 NASB).

And if you're reading these words and thinking there's no hope for you to live hearing from God because you have a tough time just reading the Bible and getting anything out of it, stop right there.

I want to encourage you. No one has even fallen in love with the Word of God accidentally or easily. But when we faithfully give ourselves to the Word of God, the Word gives back ever more faithfully, until we can't imagine how we ever lived without it. For anyone who isn't there but wants to be, I can offer you a few tried-and-true steps.

1. Ask Holy Spirit to help you hunger for the Word.
2. Go to the Word looking to be fed, not to mark it off your daily to-do list.
3. Practice articulating something you're reading or learning with someone else, however ineptly you feel you're communicating it.
4. Repeat steps one through three.

Heads up: Skipping number three will rob you and others! Don't be self-conscious because you don't have "three points and a prayer" for someone. Start wherever you are and commit to telling another breathing soul what you're reading and studying, and watch God fill you up to pour you out.

Nothing New But You

God has a unique message for the world meant to come through your one-of-a-kind life because you experience Him through your exclusive personality, experiences, and culture, etc., like no other human ever has or ever will. In dying to yourself and living to Him, you'll model your distinctive image of God in your own unique way.

Life with all of its challenges doesn't stop coming at us once we decide to find the life Jesus died to give us. To say otherwise would be an injustice. We all take direct hits we never saw coming—hits that shake us to the core and challenge everything we believe, that leave us asking, "What now?"

There's a beautiful lesson at the end of John's gospel that speaks to these "what now" moments and is one way to find our footing when we're blindsided and staggering.

In John 20:31, the author explains his goal for writing. John says he's recounted all these things so his readers would *Believe that Jesus is the Messiah, the Son of God, and that by believing you may have life in his name* (NIV). John wants us to "believe" and be "believing." That's not an accidental grammatical progression. It's how-to-move-forward language from a fellow pilgrim who knows life is going to keep coming. With his next breath, found in the opening words of John 21, the Apostle begins to tell us one last story.

The disciples are together. The setting is after the resurrection; Jesus has appeared to them more than once but hasn't yet ascended to Heaven. The Word doesn't tell us what the men are talking about, but it's hard to imagine they could get very far in any conversation without returning to the remarkable events they've just witnessed. I wonder if they were trying to figure out what to do next. Why? Because they knew how to live with the Jesus they walked with before the Cross, but now everything has changed. It's why I suspect the boys are smack dab in the middle of a "What now? Now what?" moment.

If that's so, Peter would've made a good Southern redneck boy. His conclusion in John 21:3 is short and to the point. I can see him scuffing his sandaled toe in the dust, his thoughts swirling this way and that before he takes a deliberate breath to announce, "*I'm going fishing.*" The Word says the rest of the boys replied, "*We're going, too.*" Peter, the leader.

I'd love for you to stop and read the entire account, but I'll hit some high points. John picks up the story the following morning, when Jesus finds the guys fishing. What Jesus didn't do is as instructive as what He did. For starters, He didn't chastise the disciples for going fishing. On the contrary, He rescued what had been wasted effort before He came on the scene.

Nor did He say, "You don't have any fish? That's okay. I've already got some fish on the coals." No, Jesus tells them where to fish, instructs them to add their catch to the fish and bread He's already prepared, and invites them to feast with Him. I see Resurrected Jesus speaking to their "Now what?" with an illustrated message. *He's still planning to join them in their everyday normal activities.*

Jesus didn't chastise Peter the fisherman for going back to what he knew before Jesus called him. He showed Peter, and us, how to live after we come to faith. It's not just okay for us to resume normal living, it's recommended—expected, even. Only now we're meant to live and break bread with Him in the middle of it all.

After feasting with His friends, Jesus further lays out the way forward, illustrating how His followers are to tend to the rest of His beloved people out of the nourishing relationship they have with Him. But I'm getting ahead of myself.

Let's frame the scene. In a passage familiar to many in the church, Jesus confronts Peter with the same question three times: *"Peter, do you love me more than these?"* Each time, Peter responds that Jesus knows he loves Him, and each time, Jesus points to service, telling Peter to "feed" His sheep, "tend" His sheep, and "shepherd" His lambs.

I've heard many good sermons on this passage based on different versions of the Greek word translated "love" used throughout the story, but I also find another powerful lesson here. I see Jesus emphasizing how Peter can both nurture his love for Jesus and move forward in their relationship.

The answer to Peter's "now what" is looking away from himself and tending others. It's our answer, too, because it's Who Jesus is, and He never changes. He came to serve, and He calls us to serve. The One Who set aside His divinity to rescue us asks the rescued to partner with Him to tend His loved ones. We find our way forward by dining with Him and tending others out of our life with Him, by wrenching our eyes from our lives to place them on Life

Himself, and then to give Life away. We die to ourselves every time we let Jesus cross us, break our wills, and give our lives away.

We don't learn such living in a once and done. We learn it by daring to die to us and live to Him in this moment and the next, until we realize Jesus is taking our bloated, self-centered lives and giving them purpose and meaning. When Jesus becomes our food, He becomes our life, and our life in Him becomes our conversation, and in tending others, we keep finding the way forward. The life He pours into us pours out of us because we can't contain Him. Make no mistake, the Spirit in us intends to make us broken bread and poured-out wine.

To tend God's people, we must feed on Jesus—and in feeding, we discover we must tend. The cycle continues until one day we realize we're no longer saying, "I just don't know how to live this life. I'm going fishing." Now, we're saying what Peter would later come to say in Acts 3:6: "Such as I have, give I thee."

I was on book tour once in Natchez, Mississippi, when I had a fascinating conversation with a reader. The lady talked about growing up in New Orleans, a city rich in churches and cathedrals. This woman said she grew up unchurched, but she remembered wandering into the different sanctuaries as a young woman, wondering what happened there and why it seemed to mean so much to so many.

People wander into our sanctuaries, too—your life and mine—and what has so transfixed our gaze will capture theirs. Will it be Jesus? The people who influence us the most are those who have become so addicted to gazing at this Holy Mediator between God and man that they unconsciously bid us to walk with them.

We're walking sanctuaries where others can experience God through us before they ever come to know Him for themselves. The One who created us continues to shape us. And Heaven help us with this responsibility—He has purposed our lives to shape those around us. You and I can change their world.

Forgive my bluntness, but our faith words are a dime a dozen. This world is bloated with religion but starved for Jesus. The good news is that by continually beholding Him, we can share the Bread of Life with our world. We can't give another person the joy of the Lord, but we can live magnifying Him. We can't hand them peace. But our lives can so drip with the soul peace we find in Jesus that others seek Him and find their heart's true home, their happy place. Jesus alone satiates our core while stirring our hearts to want more because through Him we're tasting eternity. We're meant to live on this Bread and offer it to others.

It's called a food chain. We've heard of them, but do we realize we're passing on what we're feeding on? Genesis tells us that once Eve ate, she gave to her husband and he ate. That's sobering. It means the conclusions we draw about what is good for food, lovely to behold, and desirable to make us wise goes far beyond our individual choices.

It may not be today, and it may not be tomorrow, but those dearest to us will benefit from being in our food chain, or they'll pay the cost of us finding our nourishment and satisfaction outside of God. What will we choose for them?

Listen to the words of Psalm 48:9-14. In Scripture, Mount Zion is used as a symbol of the City of God. As you read these words, hear God telling us to run around our new home, explore His great salvation, and then take the good news to others:

Within your temple, O God, we meditate on your unfailing love. Like your name, O God, your praise reaches to the ends of the earth; your right hand is filled with righteousness. Mount Zion rejoices, the villages of Judah are glad because of your judgments.

Walk about Zion, go around her, count her towers, consider well her ramparts, view her citadels, that you may tell of them to the next generation. For this God is our God for ever and ever; he will be our guide even to the end (Psalm 48:9-14 NIV).

God's plan for reaching the world is you and me becoming His love letters. Remember when we studied how He took His great big finger and wrote on the tablets of stone to give His commandments to the children of Israel? This same God promised a new day would come when He would take His Mighty Spirit and write His law on the hearts and minds of His children.

For this is the covenant that I will make with the house of Israel After those days, says the Lord: "I will put My laws into their minds, And I will write them on their hearts. And I will be their God, And they shall be My people.

"And they shall not teach everyone his fellow citizen, And everyone his brother, saying, 'Know the Lord,' For all will know Me, From the least to the greatest of them.

"For I will be merciful to their iniquities, And I will remember their sins no more." (Hebrews 8:10-12 NASB)

That day has come. Once we begin living the holy dare of losing us for the joy of knowing Him, we begin to bear His light for others to find their way to Him. And often through no intentional effort of our own.

Paul said, *"It is clear that you are Christ's letter, produced by us, not written with ink but with the Spirit of the living God—not on stone tablets but on tablets that are hearts of flesh."* (2 Corinthians 3:3 HCSB)

The Old Testament prophets were often called to live or act out certain messages. We're called to be the Message, to be God's love letters to the world, and we become those letters of recommendation by the transformation that happens as we behold Him.

As I've often said to my friends, we want others to see God in us, but God knows we need to see Him in ourselves first. He knows that when the Written Word, the Living Word, has begun transforming our lives, all will see Him.

Now as they observed the confidence of Peter and John and understood that they were uneducated and untrained men, they were amazed, and began to recognize them as having been with Jesus (Acts 4:13 NASB).

Transformation is powerful stuff! The culture knows it—hence the bombardment of before-and-after images in magazines and on home-improvement shows. This transformative life is our calling, and Paul encourages us to live it in Christ transparently! Be brave enough to let others follow your journey. It costs us to let others see our weaknesses, but it encourages them when they see Christ at work in us in those very things. Whether we choose to only show our strengths or only reveal our weaknesses—either way, we fail those watching.

Jesus is the most real to us and through us when we risk what someone may think of us for the greater goal of having them think about Him. When we're dying to self, we're opening the way for those around us to live to God. *So then, death is at work in us, but life in you!* (2 Corinthians 4:12 NASB) The life of one who walks with God is the life that recommends Christ to the world because such a life manifests the power of God. The hearts of those around us hunger for the reality of God, just like we do. We're meant to be a catalyst.

We are His, and He is ours. Out of our union, He calls them. From our hearts, He loves them, and they draw nearer. From our lives, they seek shelter and draw closer still until we are no more, and He is standing before them. And they become His, and He becomes theirs.

I leave you with a few lines of prose and the sincere hope that our time together will help you find the deep and wide life Jesus died to give you…

> *Because of Who He Is*
> *Look at me, what do you see?*
> *A mama, daughter, wife and grand,*
> *sister, soldier, friend?*
> *I'm all of that, do all of that,*
> *live all of that, love all of that.*
>
> *It's what you don't see that defines me.*
> *I'm Heaven-sought, blood-bought, Spirit-taught.*
> *In me is Life that never dies,*
> *joy that defies, and love realized.*

These feet walk on dusty ground
but this soul is Heaven bound.
I was lost and I am found,
left here now to astound,
in trials, triumphs, peace and pain
joy, sorrow, loss and gain.

A goal, so great, I can't obtain,
though fits and spurts I may can feign.
All my efforts to abstain,
every struggle, every strain,
wrecks the lie of little "i,"
and proves again I cannot live
unless I die.

Lasting change, for this I plead
more proof, less creed
is what I need.
On shaky knees I hear His voice
reminding me I have a choice.
I can listen to hear,
hear to obey, obey to abide,
abide to be transformed,
and be transformed
that I might reveal His glory.
Your mission is mine if He is yours,
not because of who we are,
but because of Who. He. Is.

~SHELLIE RUSHING TOMLINSON

Questions for Group Study or Private Reflection

1. In your own words, record Shellie's suggestions for learning to love the Bible. Do you find one more challenging than the others? Why?

2. Do you agree with Shellie's assertion that everyone has a God story and an opportunity to bear His image in a unique way? If so, and you have the faintest idea what yours might be, record it here.

3. Have you learned something in this chapter you could articulate to someone else? What is that?

Acknowledgements

It never fails. Whenever I set out to write acknowledgements, I hear the countdown music start playing and I feel the pressure of getting everything in before I'm escorted to the wings. In my head I know that happens on award shows and not in print, but apparently this soothing news never travels to my stomach. I want to thank everyone responsible for this book existing, but I'm super nervous I may leave someone out! (Again, the awards show thing. But the music is playing, so here we go.)

To the women of Providence Church who let me teach on this deep and wide life before it ever grew into a book, and for your helpful input along the way. Thank you.

To my immediate family and friends, thank you for all the times you heard, "I'm sorry, I need to write today" without throwing something at my head. It was hurting enough trying to get these words out.

To Greg Johnson, Super-Agent, I truly appreciate your continuing to represent my work to people who can get it to the page. In my imagination, your opening to them reads something like, "I've got this one author ... She's a trip, but her love for Jesus is genuine. Here's her latest for your consideration ..." Thank you.

To Tim Peterson, thank you for seeing the potential of *Finding Deep and Wide*, for wanting it for your list, and for the encouraging phone calls that never failed to lower my author angst. That's something of a miracle right there. (And thanks for letting me color outside the lines with the cover thing.)

To Karla Dial, only you and I know how often your wise editing saved this manuscript when I was rambling ad nauseum or driving off into a well-meaning ditch. If I had my way, I'd never write another book, email, social media post, or text without your input. Enough said.

To Jessica Maher, cover designer. I realize this is an unusual acknowledgement to find here, but when have I ever been normal? (Don't answer that.) Thank you for seeing my heart for this book and being willing to offer your incredible design services to our team during my micromanaging madness. The fact that you're also my daughter? Pure gravy.

To Phil, my beloved farmer, and my favorite human. My appreciation for you would take a book of its own to express. God knew it would take an incredibly special someone to put up with me. For a man of few words, you support both my weirdness and my wordiness with a steadfast love that looks a lot like Father's. I thank you and I love you beyond.

And, of course, my sweet Jesus. I close with Your Name in the hope that it has the prominence You deserve. I'll never understand why You chose me for salvation, why You're faithfully forming Your Life in mine, and why You allow me to speak for You and of You to the world. You and I know the road we've traveled and how unfit I am for the job, today and every day, apart from You. May my life demonstrate gratitude in a way that brings You much glory.

Yours,
Shellie

About the Author

Hey y'all!

I love connecting with readers. Find me on Facebook, follow me on Twitter, or swap pics with me on Instagram and Pinterest, and let's stay in touch. All those social links can be found at my website, belleofallthingssouthern.com. Not into social media? Email me at tomtom@allthingssouthern.com or send me an actual letter (anyone remember those?) to 610 Schneider Lane, Lake Providence, LA 71254.

Do you participate in a book club or Bible study group? I'd love to connect with you and your friends. Contact me and we'll make it happen. You're also invited to join me on the All Things Southern podcast. It's available at iTunes, Spotify, and Google Play, or you can just hit the audio links at the website when a new episode drops. Again, that's belleofallthingssouthern.com or ShellieRushingTomlinson.com.

If you've enjoyed *Finding Deep and Wide*, would you consider reviewing it on a site like Amazon, Goodreads, or Christianbook.com? Those reviews help share the message more than you can imagine. Many, many thanks! Let's stay in touch and keep seeking this Jesus together, forever. He is worthy.

Hugs,
Shellie

ALSO BY SHELLIE RUSHING TOMLINSON

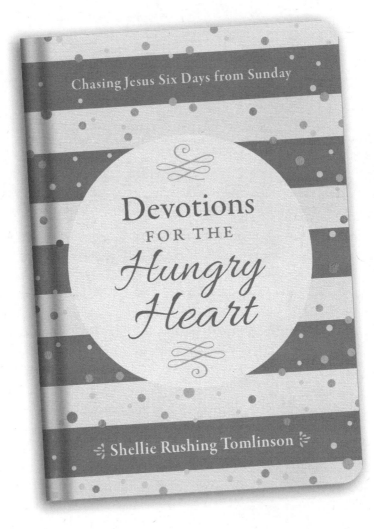

Devotions for the Hungry Heart

Chasing Jesus Six Days from Sunday

272 pages | ISBN-13: 978-1683224327

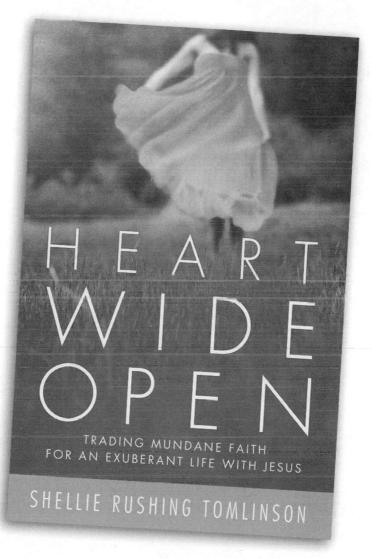

Heart Wide Open

Trading Mundane Faith for an Exuberant Life with Jesus

208 pages | ISBN-13: 978-0307731937

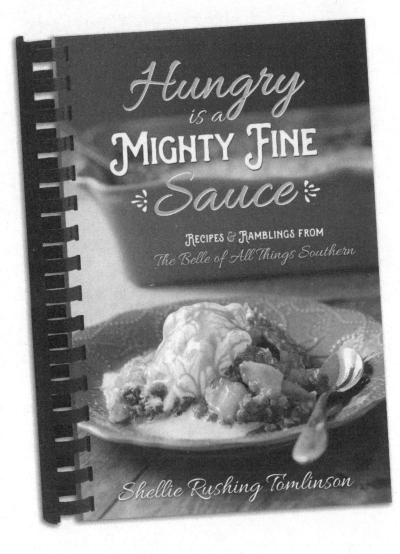

Hungry Is a Mighty Fine Sauce Cookbook

Recipes and Ramblings from the Belle of All Things Southern

224 pages | ISBN-13: 978-1634097826

*Suck Your Stomach In
& Put Some
Color On!*

**What Southern Mamas
Tell their Daughters that
the Rest of Y'all Should
Know Too**

Shellie Rushing
Tomlinson
Host of *All Things Southern*

Suck Your Stomach in and Put Some Color On!

What Southern Mamas Tell Their Daughters that the Rest of Y'all Should Know Too

304 pages | ISBN-13: 978-0425221341

"Laugh-out-loud funny."
—Jeff Foxworthy

Sue Ellen's Girl Ain't Fat, She Just Weighs Heavy

The Belle of All Things Southern Dishes on Men, Money, and Not Losing Your Midlife Mind

Shellie Rushing Tomlinson
National Bestselling Author of Suck Your Stomach In & Put Some Color On!

Sue Ellen's Girl Ain't Fat, She Just Weighs Heavy

The Belle of All Things Southern Dishes on Men, Money, and Not Losing Your Midlife Mind

336 pages | ISBN-13: 978-0425240854